Using
Microsoft Excel

2023 Edition

Kevin Wilson

www.elluminetpress.com

Using Microsoft Excel - 2023 Edition

Publisher: Elluminet Press
Director: Kevin Wilson
Lead Editor: Steven Ashmore
Technical Reviewer: Mike Taylor, Robert Ashcroft
Copy Editors: Joanne Taylor, James Marsh
Proof Reader: Mike Taylor
Indexer: James Marsh
Cover Designer: Kevin Wilson

eBook versions and licenses are also available for most titles. Any source code or other supplementary materials referenced by the author in this text is available to readers at

www.elluminetpress.com/resources

For detailed information about how to locate your book's resources, go to

www.elluminetpress.com/resources

Table of Contents

About the Author

With over 20 years' experience in the computer industry, Kevin Wilson has made a career out of technology and showing others how to use it. After earning a master's degree in computer science, software engineering, and multimedia systems, Kevin has held various positions in the IT industry including graphic & web design, digital film & photography, programming & software engineering, developing & managing corporate networks, building computer systems, and IT support.

He serves as senior writer and director at Elluminet Press Ltd, he periodically teaches computer science at college, and works as an IT trainer in England while researching for his PhD. His books have become a valuable resource among the students in England, South Africa, Canada, and in the United States.

Kevin's motto is clear: "If you can't explain something simply, then you haven't understood it well enough." To that end, he wrote the Exploring Tech Computing series, in which he breaks down complex technological subjects into smaller, easy-to-follow steps that students and ordinary computer users can put into practice.

Microsoft Excel

Microsoft Excel, commonly known as Excel, is a spreadsheet application that is part of the Microsoft Office suite, originally launched in 1985. Over the years, Excel has become an indispensable tool that is used in various industries, including finance, marketing, business, academia, and even personal use. It serves as a versatile platform for storing, organizing, analyzing, and manipulating numerical data, which can be presented in either tabular or graphical formats.

Before we begin, throughout this book, we will be using the resource files.

You can download these files from

`elluminetpress.com/excel`

To begin lets explore what a spreadsheet is.

What is a Spreadsheet?

A spreadsheet is a software application that enables users to organize analyse, and store data in tabular format. The spreadsheet itself is made up of rows and columns of cells, where each cell can hold individual data such as numbers, text, currency, and dates.

Each cell is identified by a reference. The reference is made up by using the column, eg D, followed by the row, eg 10.

[COLUMN] [ROW]

So for example, the highlighted cell in the illustration below would be D10.

You can also select multiple cells at the same time. A group of cells is called as a cell range. You can refer to a cell range, using the cell reference of the first cell and the last cell in the range, separated by a colon.

[FIRST CELL in RANGE] : [LAST CELL in RANGE]

For example in the illustration below, this cell range would be A1:D10 (firstcell : lastcell).

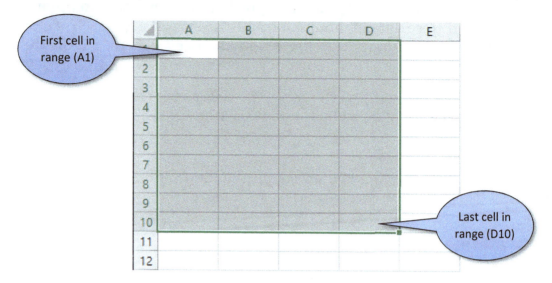

Cell references are used when you start applying functions to the numbers in your cells. In the example below, to add two numbers together, you can enter a formula into cell C1.

Instead of typing in **=5+5** you would enter **=A1+B1**.

The theory is, if you enter the cell reference instead of the actual number, you can perform calculations automatically, and Excel will recalculate all the numbers for you should you change anything.

For example, if I wanted to change it to **5+6**, I would just change the number in cell B1 without rewriting the formula in C1.

Now you can type any number in either cell A1 or B1 and it will add them up automatically.

This is a very basic example but forms the building blocks of a spreadsheet. You can use these concepts to build spreadsheets to analyse and manipulate data, as well as allow changes to the individual data and other parts of the spreadsheet without constantly changing formulas and functions.

You can analyse your data using pivot tables, goal seek and scenario manager. Pivot tables allow users to summarize and analyze large amounts of data quickly and easily. Goal Seek allows users to determine the input value needed to achieve a specific output value in a formula. Scenario Manager is a tool that allows users to create and compare different scenarios based on changes to input values.

Recommended Retail Price			Sale Price			Give Away Price		
Revenues			**Revenues**			**Revenues**		
Price per Book	£	14.95	Price per Book	£	10.95	Price per Book	£	8.99
Book Sales		50	Book Sales		50	Book Sales		50
Total revenue	£	747.50	**Total revenue**	£	547.50	**Total revenue**	£	449.50
Expenditure			**Expenditure**			**Expenditure**		
RRP		14.95	RRP		14.95	RRP		14.95
Discount		55%	Discount		55%	Discount		55%
Wholesale Price	£	6.73	Wholesale Price	£	6.73	Wholesale Price	£	6.73
Total Stock		50	Total Stock		50	Total Stock		50
Total Cost	£	336.38	**Total Cost**	£	336.38	**Total Cost**	£	336.38
Profit Margin	£	411.13	**Profit Margin**	£	211.13	**Profit Margin**	£	113.13

You can also create charts to visually represent your data. Excel charts are visual representations of data that can help users better understand and analyze information within a spreadsheet.

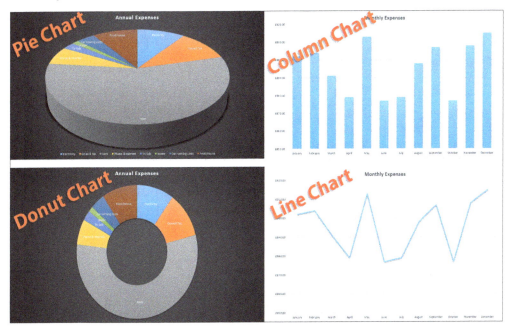

Excel provides a variety of chart types, including column charts, line charts, pie charts, bar charts, area charts, and scatter charts.

2

Getting Started

In this chapter, we'll explore the functionalities and mechanics of the Microsoft Excel interface We'll look at:

- Getting Started
- Starting Excel
- Main Screen
- The Ribbon
- Home Ribbon Tab
- Insert Ribbon Tab
- Page Layout Ribbon Tab
- Formulas Ribbon Tab
- Data Ribbon Tab
- Review Ribbon Tab
- View Ribbon Tab
- Quick Access Toolbar
- File Backstage
- Tell Me Feature
- Workbooks and Worksheets

To help you better understand this section, take a look at the video resources. Open your web browser and navigate to the following website:

elluminetpress.com/start-excel

Starting Excel

The quickest way to start Microsoft Excel is to search for it using the search field on the bottom left of your task bar. Type 'excel' into the search field. From the search results click 'excel'. You'll also find Excel on your start menu.

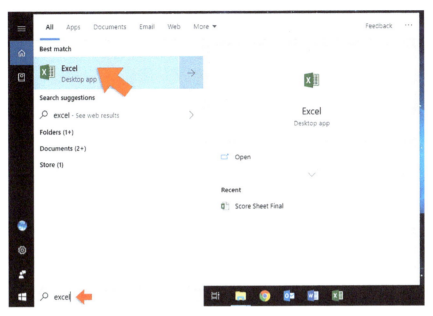

Once Excel has started, you'll land on the home screen. On the home screen, you'll see recently used templates along the top, and your most recently saved spreadsheets listed underneath.

To begin, click 'blank workbook' to start. This will open up Excel with a new spreadsheet for you.

Main Screen

Once you have selected a template, you will see your main screen.

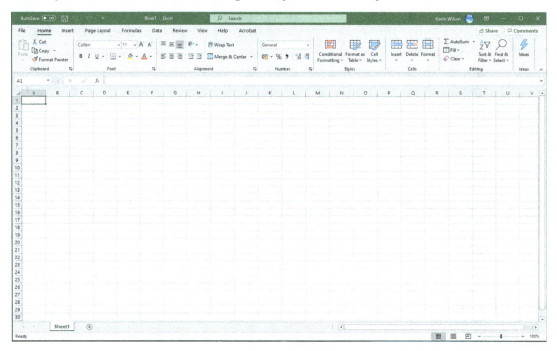

Your columns are labelled across the top of your worksheet with letters and your rows are labelled down the left hand side with numbers. These make up cell references that we'll look at later.

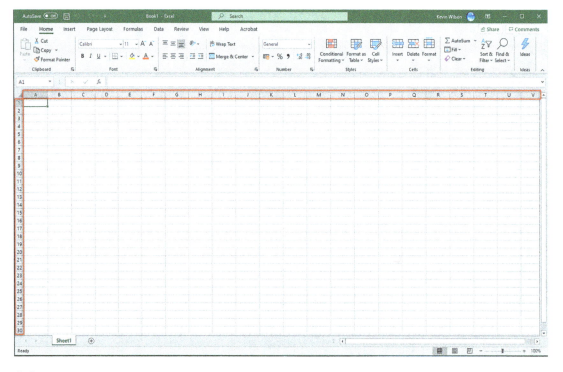

Underneath the ribbon menu, you'll see a cell reference and next to that the formula bar.

Across the bottom of the screen on the left hand side, you'll see some tabs. This shows you all the worksheets you have created in your workbook - you can click these to switch to that worksheet. You can create a new worksheet here, if you click the small plus icon next to the tabs.

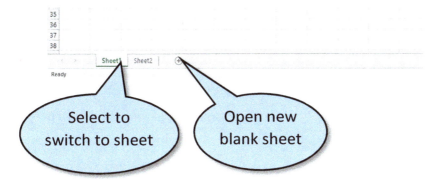

On the bottom right, you can change how Excel displays your worksheet. Grid view is your normal view as shown above, print view shows you how your spreadsheet will look when printed.

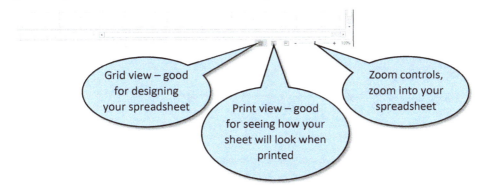

Further to the right you have your zoom controls. This allows you to zoom in and out of your spreadsheet.

Chapter 2: Getting Started

You can either use the slider to zoom in and out, or you can click on the 'zoom percentage' on the bottom right.

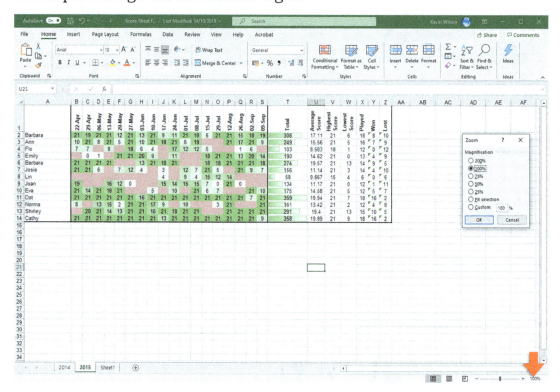

From the 'zoom' dialog box that appears, you can select the zoom level.

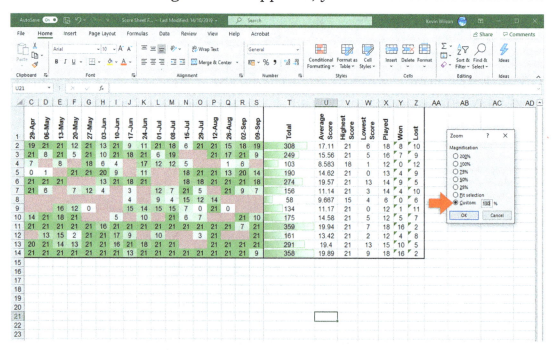

Click 'ok' when you're done.

The Ribbon

All the tools used in Microsoft Excel are organised into a ribbon which is divided into ribbon tabs, each containing a specific set of tools.

The most used ribbon tabs are home, insert and formulas. For normal use of Excel, these are the ones you will be looking in the most detail.

Home Ribbon Tab

This is where you will find your most used tools for basic text formatting, cell borders, cell formatting for text and numbers or currency, etc.

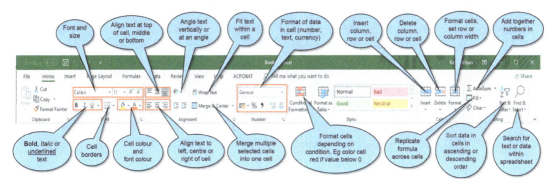

Insert Ribbon Tab

This is where you will find all your objects that you can insert into your spreadsheet, such as shapes, tables and charts.

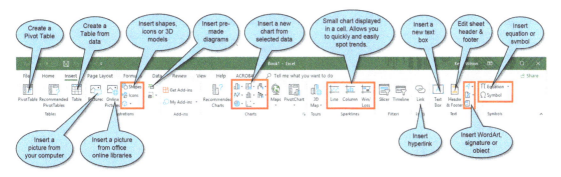

You can also insert equations and symbols, as well as pivot tables and pivot charts.

Page Layout Ribbon Tab

This is where you will find your page formatting functions, such as size of paper, colors & themes, paper orientation when printed, paper margins, etc.

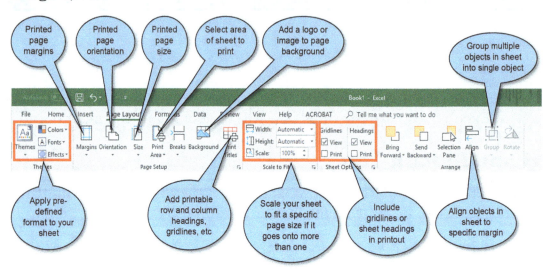

Formulas Ribbon Tab

This is where you will find your formulas, functions and your data manipulation tools. Sum functions, average, counting tools, etc.

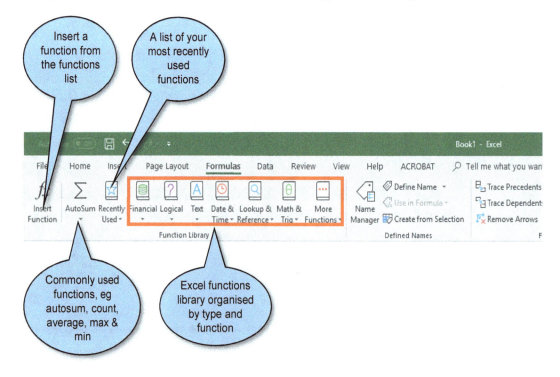

Data Ribbon Tab

The data ribbon is where you can find tools to connect to external data sources and databases, as well as sort data.

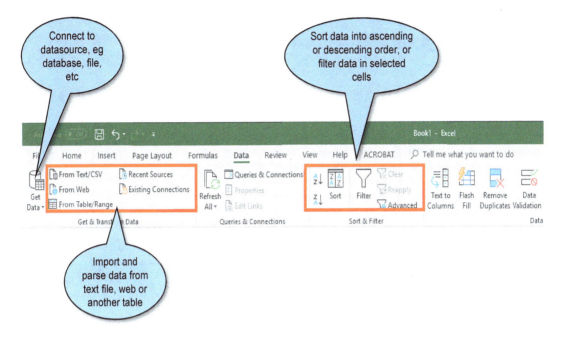

Review Ribbon Tab

The review ribbon has tools that allow you to add comments as well as check spelling and protect parts of the spreadsheet from making changes.

View Ribbon Tab

This is where you will find your view layouts, where you can zoom into your spreadsheet etc.

Quick Access Toolbar

The Quick Access Toolbar provides quick and easy access to frequently used commands and functions with just a click. You'll find it on the top left of the title bar in the main window.

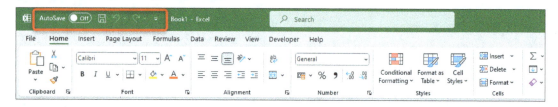

By default, the Quick Access Toolbar contains only a few commonly used commands such as Save, Undo, and Redo.

If you want to add a command, right-click on any command in the ribbon then select 'Add to Quick Access Toolbar'. For example, if you wanted to add the 'macros' command from the 'developer' ribbon.

You'll see the command appear on the toolbar.

If you want to remove a command, right-click on it and choose "Remove from Quick Access Toolbar."

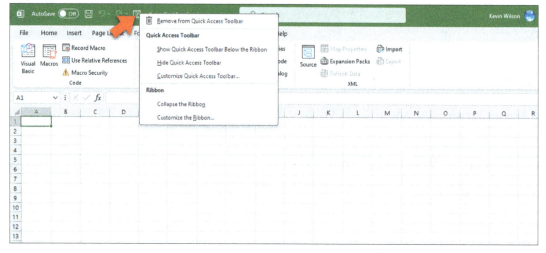

File Backstage

If you click 'File' on the top left of your screen, this will open up what Microsoft call the backstage.

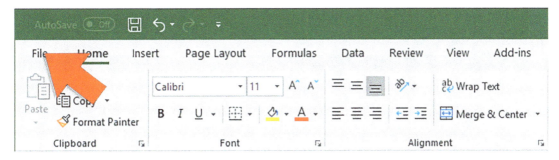

Backstage is where you open or save spreadsheets and workbooks, print, export or share workbooks, as well as options, Microsoft account and preference settings.

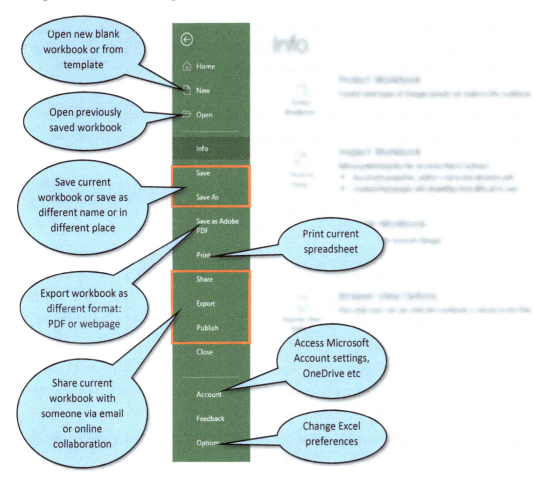

You can also change your Microsoft Account settings, log in and activate your Microsoft Office, change Excel's preferences and so on.

Tell Me Feature

Microsoft has added a feature to Office that allows you to search for commands and tools in any of the Office Applications.

You can find this field on the top right of the screen. Here it is pictured in Excel.

Type a command in to the field. For example, if I wanted to insert a picture, type 'insert picture' into the search field.

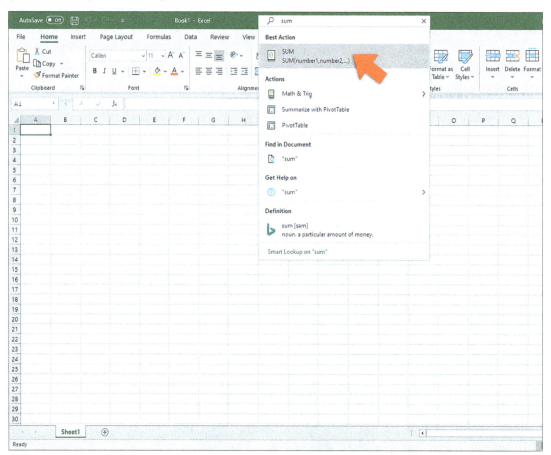

From the drop down menu that appears, click on the command you were looking for.

This feature can be used in all the Office Apps. If you can't find the tool on the menus or ribbons, just search for it.

Workbooks and Worksheets

In Microsoft Excel, "workbook" and "worksheet" are two fundamental terms that refer to different components of the application. Lets take a look at what they mean.

Workbook

A workbook is the primary document in Excel. It can be thought of as a container that holds all your Excel worksheets, charts, and other elements.

A single Excel workbook typically has a file extension of ".xlsx" (for modern Excel versions) or ".xls" (for older versions).

A workbook can contain one or more worksheets.

Worksheet

A worksheet, often referred to as a "sheet", is an individual tab or page within an Excel workbook. Each worksheet is a spreadsheet consisting of a grid of cells organized in rows and columns.

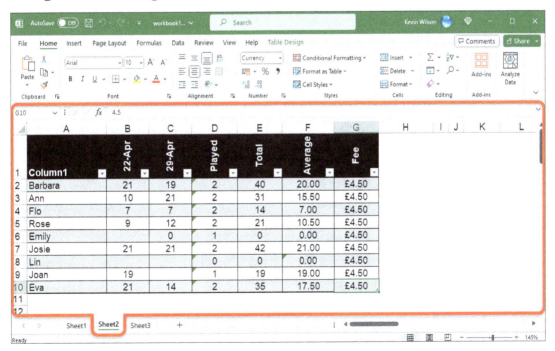

Excel worksheets appear along the bottom of the workbook as tabs. By default Excel names these tabs 'sheet1', 'sheet2', 'sheet3' and so on, but you can rename these to more meaningful names.

3

Building Spreadsheets

In this chapter, we'll explore how to create spreadsheets, edit and format text. We'll look at:

- Building Spreadsheets
- Creating a New Workbook
- Simple Text Formatting
- Inserting Rows & Columns
- Cut, Copy, Paste and Paste Special
- Sorting Data
- Formatting your Spreadsheet
- Cell Alignment, formatting & borders
- Opening a New Sheet
- Copy Data Between Sheets
- Freeze Panes
- Split Screen
- Importing Data
- Conditional Formatting
- Using Multiple Workbooks

To help you better understand this section, take a look at the video resources. Open your web browser and navigate to the following website:

elluminetpress.com/exc-docs

You'll also need to download the source files from:

elluminetpress.com/excel

Creating a New Workbook

To create a new blank workbook, click 'file' on the top left of your screen,

Select 'new', then double click the 'blank workbook' thumbnail.

You'll see a blank spreadsheet where you can start to enter your data.

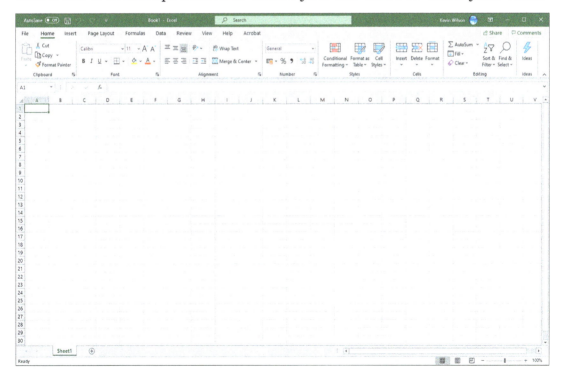

Now we can start entering our data.

Entering Data

In this example we are doing a basic scoring sheet. To enter data, click on the cell you want, then type in the data.

	A	B	C	D
1		22-Apr	29-Apr	Total
2	Barbara	21	19	
3	Ann	10	21	
4	Flo	7	7	
5	Rose	9	12	
6	Emily		0	
7	Josie	21	21	
8	Lin			
9	Joan	19		
10	Eva	21	14	
11				

Simple Text Formatting

Sometimes it improves the readability of your spreadsheet to format the data in the cells.

For example, make the heading rows bold.

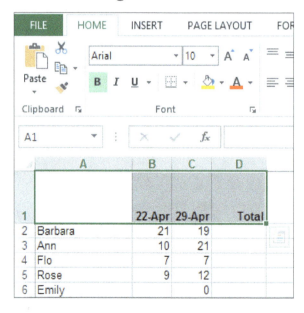

You can do this by selecting the heading row as shown above and click the bold icon.

Text Orientation

Now because the headings are quite long and take up a lot of space, you can change the orientation of the headings to read vertically instead of horizontally. This helps save space and looks better when printed on a page.

To do this, select the cells you want to change the orientation of. Then right click your mouse on the selection. From the menu that appears, select 'format cells'.

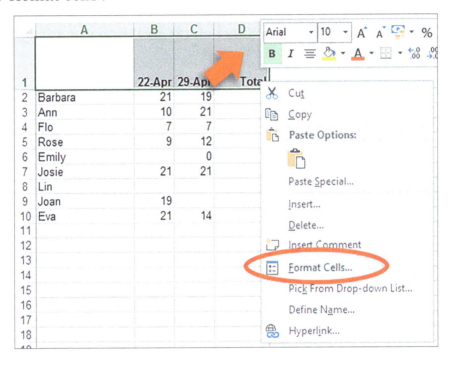

In the dialog box, click the alignment tab. From there, go to the orientation section on the right of the dialog box.

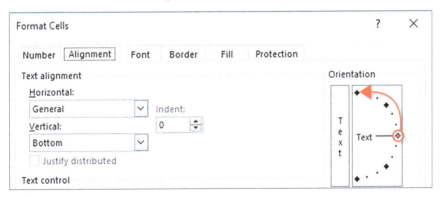

Click the horizontal point (circled above) and drag it up to the top (the vertical point). Or you can enter 90 in the degrees box.

You will see the headings are now oriented vertically.

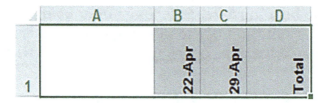

Resizing Rows and Columns

You can resize a column or row by clicking and dragging the column or row divider lines as circled below

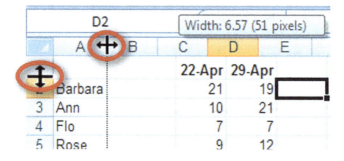

You can also double click on these lines to automatically size the row or column to the data that is in the cell.

Inserting Rows & Columns

To insert a row between Flo and Rose, right click with your mouse on the row Rose is in. In this case row 5

	A	B 22-Apr	C 29-Apr	D Total
1				
2	Barbara	21	19	
3	Ann	10	21	
4	Flo	7	7	
5	Rose	9	12	
6	Emily		0	
7	Josie	21	21	
8	Lin			
9	Joan	19		
10	Eva	21	14	

A5 — Rose

From the menu, click insert. This will insert a blank row above Rose.

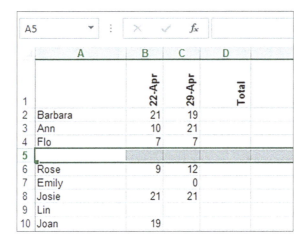

Here we can see Excel has inserted a blank row between the players Flo and Rose.

	A	22-Apr (B)	29-Apr (C)	Total (D)
1				
2	Barbara	21	19	
3	Ann	10	21	
4	Flo	7	7	
5				
6	Rose	9	12	
7	Emily		0	
8	Josie	21	21	
9	Lin			
10	Joan	19		

Remember, the new row is always added above the one selected, and a new column is always added before the one selected.

To insert a column it is exactly the same procedure, except you select a column instead of a row.

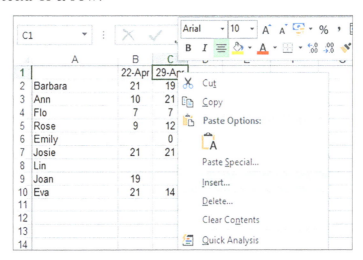

Cut, Copy & Paste

You can copy and paste a cell or cell range and paste it into another worksheet/workbook or in a different location on the same worksheet.

For this example, open **Score Sheet Final.xlsx**. To perform a basic copy, select the cells you want to copy, and from your home ribbon, click copy.

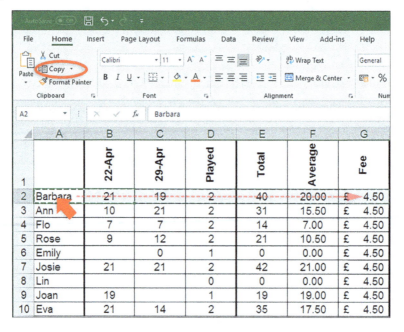

Click the cell where you want the cells to be copied to. I'm going to paste the cells at the end of the table. From your home ribbon, click paste.

Paste Special

By default, Excel pastes everything copied from the selected cells. Sometimes you only want to paste certain things, such as formatting, or just the text or just the formulas. You can do this with the 'paste special' feature. To find 'paste special', click the small down arrow under the 'paste' icon, on your home ribbon.

You'll see a drop down menu with a few options, shown in the illustrations below. For example, to paste only the formulas, click the second icon across (*fx*).

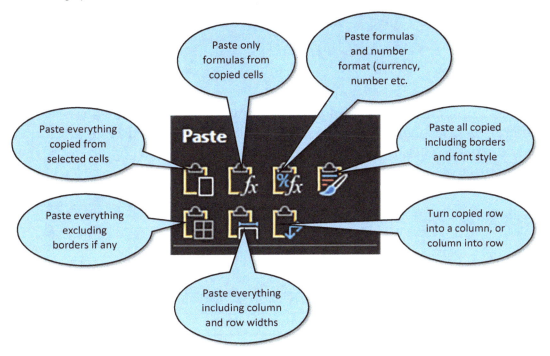

If you just want the values, look further down the drop down menu to the values section, and click '123'.

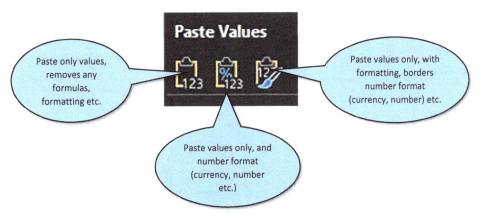

Finally, if you just want the formatting such as the cell borders and number formatting (ie currency, number, text etc), then further down the drop down menu, you'll find the 'other paste options' section. To only paste the formatting, click the first option (%).

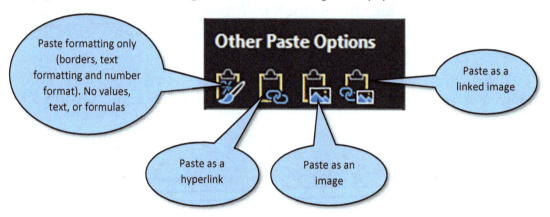

Paste as link can be useful if you are copying and pasting values from a different worksheet to a summarised table. The pasted cells are linked to the copied cells. So if you change the values in the copied cells, they will change in the pasted cells.

	A	22-Apr	29-Apr	Played	Total	Average
1						
2	Barbara	3	19	2	22	11.00
3	Ann	10	21	2	31	15.50
4	Flo	7	7	2	14	7.00
5	Rose	9	12	2	21	10.50
6	Emily		0	1	0	0.00
7	Josie	21	21	2	42	21.00
8	Lin			0	0	0.00
9	Joan	19		1	19	19.00
10	Eva	21	14	2	35	17.50
11						
12						
13	Barbara	3	19	2	22	11

Using 'cut' is exactly the same, except select 'cut' from the home ribbon, instead of 'copy'. The cut command moves the selected cells rather than copying them.

Sorting Data

To quick sort your data, click on a cell in the column you want to sort the data by. In this example, I want to sort the data by total score so I can see who won this year's player of the year.

Click in the 'total' column. Make sure you click one of the numbers as we want to sort the data, not the title.

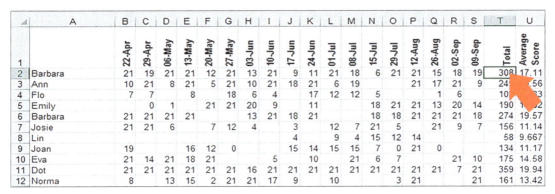

From your home ribbon, click 'sort & filter'. From the drop down menu, click 'Largest to Smallest' (descending order), as we want the highest score listed first.

Looks like Dot won this one...

	22-Apr	29-Apr	06-May	13-May	20-May	27-May	03-Jun	10-Jun	17-Jun	24-Jun	01-Jul	08-Jul	15-Jul	29-Jul	12-Aug	26-Aug	02-Sep	09-Sep	Total	Average Score	Highest Score	Lowest Score	Played	Won	Lost
Dot	21	21	21	21	21	21	16	21	21	21	21	21	21	21	21	21	7	21	359	19.94	21	7	18	16	2
Cathy	21	21	21	21	21	21	21	21	13	21	21	21	21	21	21	21	21	9	358	19.89	21	9	18	16	2
Barbara	21	19	21	21	12	21	13	21	9	11	21	18	6	21	21	15	18	19	308	17.11	21	6	18	8	10
Shirley		20	21	14	13	21	21	16	21	18	21	21			21	21	21	21	291	19.4	21	13	15	10	5
Barbara	21	21	21	21			13	21	18	21		18	18	21	21	21	18		274	19.57	21	13	14	9	5
Ann	10	21	8	21	5	21	10	21	18	21	6	19			21	17	21	9	249	15.56	21	5	16	7	9
Emily		0	1		21	21	20	9		11			18	21	21	13	20	14	190	14.62	21	0	13	4	9
Eva	21	14	21	18	21			5		10		21	6	7		21	10		175	14.58	21	5	12	5	7
Norma	8		13	15	2	21	21	17	9		10			3	21			21	161	13.42	21	2	12	4	8
Josie	21	21	6		7	12	4		3		12	7	21	5		21	9	7	156	11.14	21	3	14	4	10
Joan	19			16	12	0		15	14	15	15	7	0	21	0				134	11.17	21	0	13	4	9
Flo	7	7		8		18	6	4		17	12	12	5			1	6		103	8.583	18	1	12	0	12
Lin								4		9	4	15	12	14					58	9.667	15	4	6	0	6

The procedure is the same for 'smallest to largest' (ascending order), except click 'Smallest to Largest' from the drop down menu.

Formatting your Spreadsheet

To emphasise certain parts of your spreadsheet such as totals or headings you can apply borders and shading to cells or groups of cells.

Cell Alignment

This helps to align your data inside your cells and make it easier to read. To do this highlight the cells you want to apply the alignment to, then select 'centre' from the alignment icons highlighted above. The top three align vertically in the cell, the bottom three align horizontally in the cell.

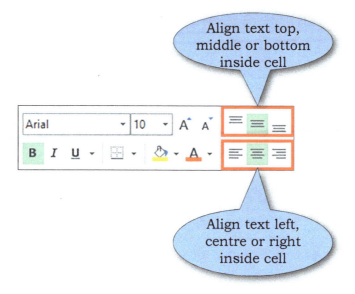

Text Format

As well as aligning the text inside your cell, you can apply bold or italic effects to make certain parts such as headings stand out.

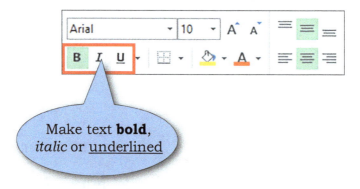

You can also change the font and size.

To do this in our spreadsheet highlight the headings ('22-Apr' to 'Fee Paid') and then click the bold icon highlighted below.

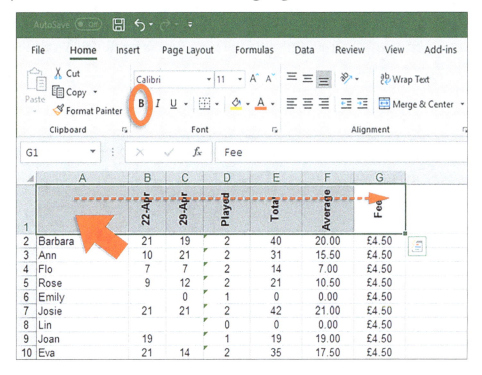

To align your text in the cells in the centre, select the cells you want then click the centre icon as highlighted below. *The top three icons align the text vertically, and the bottom three icons align the text horizontally.*

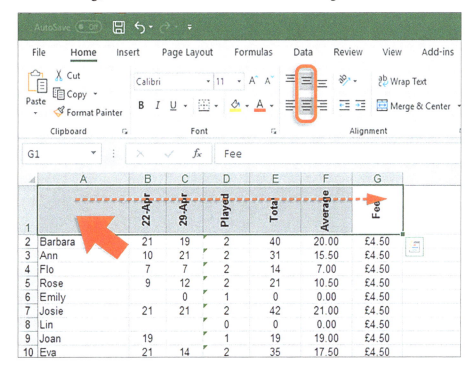

Cell Borders

To apply borders to your spreadsheet, select with your mouse the cells you want to format. In this case, I am going to do the whole table. Right click on the selected cells and select 'format cells' from the menu.

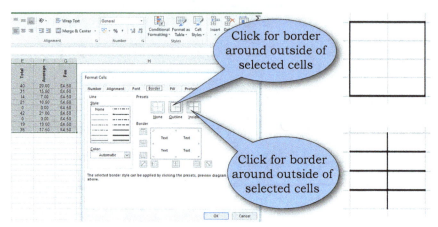

I want the borders around all the cells both inside and the outline. So from the dialog box click 'outline' & 'inside'.

Now you can tweak the borders around the cells. It would make our spreadsheet easier to read if we divided the table into sections. Player name can be one section, scores can be the second section, total, average, and fee can be the third section. We can divide the table with a thicker line. First, highlight the total, average and fee paid columns, because this is one section. Right click, select 'format cells'.

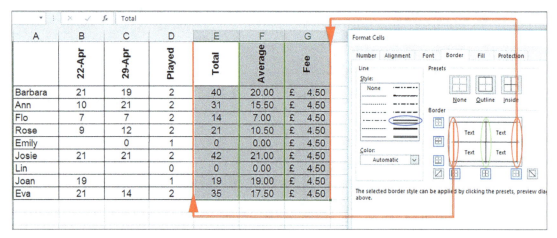

From the dialog box, under the style section, select the size of your line, circled above in blue. Under the 'border section', select the left line and the right line, circled in red above, to apply the border to these edges.

Do this with the player names column too.

First, highlight the column as shown below. Right click on the grey selection and select 'format cells' from the menu...

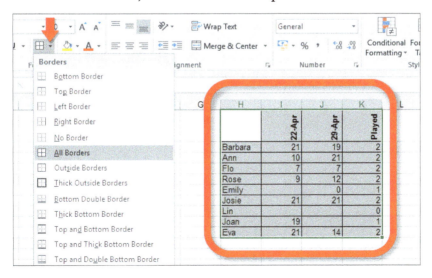

From the 'style' section of the dialog box, select the style of line, eg dotted line, solid line, thick line etc. I'm going to click the thicker line in this example, circled above in blue.

Then from the 'border section', select the right line, circled in red above, to apply the border to the right edge of the selected column.

You can quickly apply borders using the borders icon on the home ribbon. This allows you to apply common border presets. Select your cells, then click the small down arrow next to the borders icon, indicated with the red arrow below, to reveal the drop down menu.

From the drop down menu select the border you want.

Opening a New Sheet

Within your excel workbook, you can open more then one spreadsheet. To do this, click the '+' icon on the bottom left of your screen.

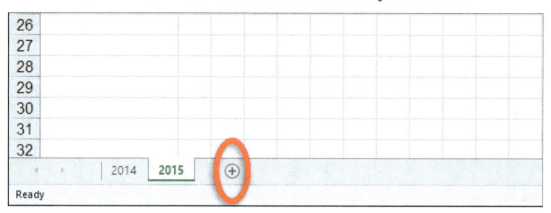

You'll see another blank tab appear along the bottom

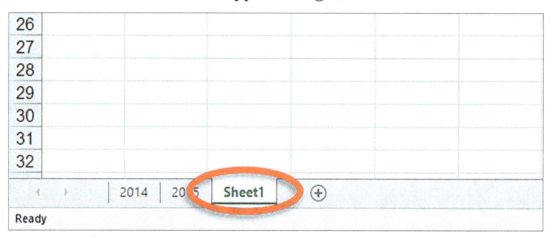

Double click on the name of the sheet, 'sheet1' in this case, and enter a meaningful name.

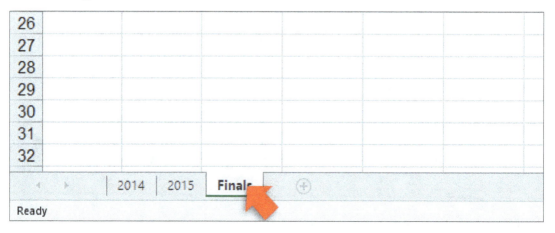

Copy Data Between Sheets

You can copy data between sheets using simple copy and paste. This works with simple data such as a name or number.

If you have formulas in the cells you want to copy, this poses more of a problem, as standard copy and paste will only copy the formula itself and you will get a "!REF" error. To get around this problem, you need to use the paste link feature.

To demonstrate this, I'm going to copy the list of names using standard copy and paste from one sheet to another. We're going to use the sample **Score Sheet Final.xlsx**.

First highlight the list of names.

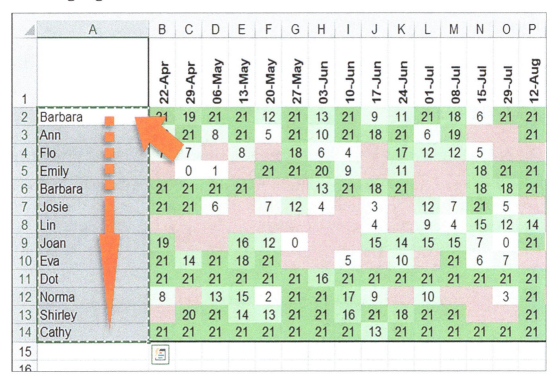

From the home ribbon, select 'copy'.

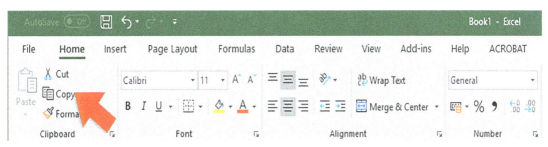

Chapter 3: Building Spreadsheets

Switch to the other sheet. Select the tab along the bottom of the screen.

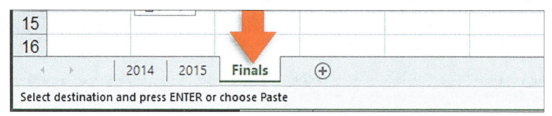

Select cell A1 (where you want the names to appear).

Select 'paste' from the home ribbon.

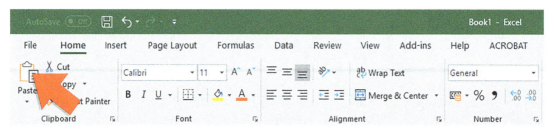

Now, I want to add a second column to contain the total scores. I don't just want to copy the values, I want to copy the formulas, so the values update as the spreadsheet is updated.

	A	B	C
1	Barbara		
2	Ann		
3	Flo		
4	Emily		
5	Barbara		
6	Josie		
7	Lin		
8	Joan		
9	Eva		
10	Dot		
11	Norma		

To do this, go back to the '2015' sheet, in the example workbook **Score Sheet Final.xlsx**.

Highlight the totals as shown below and select copy from the home ribbon.

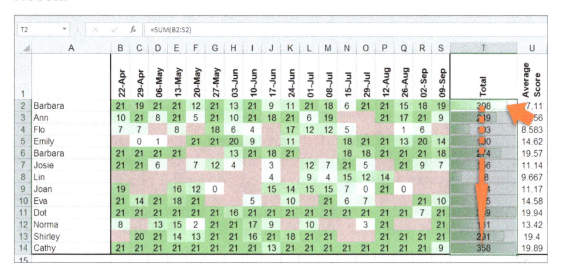

Switch to your other sheet: 'finals' and select the cell you want the values to start. In this case cell B1.

Click the down arrow under the 'paste' icon and select 'paste special'.

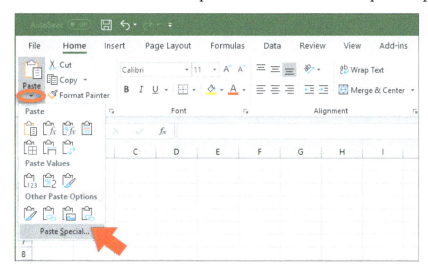

From bottom left of the dialog box select 'paste link'.

Freeze Panes

Large tables or long lists of data can often be difficult to read on a computer screen, sometimes scrolling down the list you can lose track of headings. To combat this, Excel has a feature that allows you to freeze a row or column, meaning the row/column will be on the screen at all times while you scroll down or across your screen. This is called 'freeze panes'.

If we have a look at our imported bank statement, **statement final.xls**, from the previous section, the list is quite long. Download and use the file **statement example.xls** if you haven't done the previous section.

It would be far easier to read if we froze the top row. To do this, go to your view ribbon and click 'freeze panes'. From the drop down menu, select 'freeze top row'. The top row of the list contains the headings.

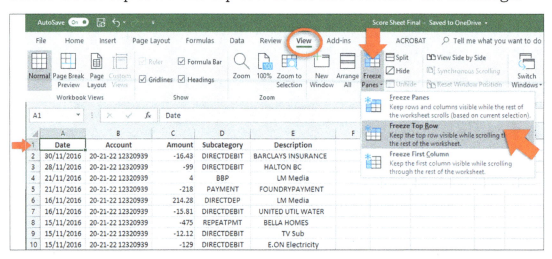

Now when you scroll down the list, the top row remains visible.

	A	B	C	D	E
1	Date	Account	Amount	Subcategory	Description
7	16/11/2016	20-21-22 12320939	-15.81	DIRECTDEBIT	UNITED UTIL WATER
8	15/11/2016	20-21-22 12320939	-475	REPEATPMT	BELLA HOMES
9	15/11/2016	20-21-22 12320939	-12.12	DIRECTDEBIT	TV Sub
10	15/11/2016	20-21-22 12320939	-129	DIRECTDEBIT	E.ON Electricity
11	14/11/2016	20-21-22 12320939	700	BBP	LM Media

You can do the same with the first column. Click 'freeze first column' instead, from the drop down menu.

In the score sheet example, if I wanted the column with the player names as well as the dates to remain visible, you can do this with freeze panes.

I have included the file **score sheet final.xls** for you to practice with. You can download the file from

elluminetpress.com/excel

When you click 'freeze panes' from the 'freeze panes' drop down menu, Excel will apply the freeze to the <u>rows above</u> and the <u>columns to the left</u> of the cell you have selected.

	22-Apr	29-Apr	06-May	13-May	20-May	27-May	03-Jun	10-Jun	17-Jun	24-Jun	01-Jul	08-Jul
Barbara	21	19	21	21	12	21	13	21	9	11	21	18
Ann	10	21	8	21	5	21	10	21	18	21	6	19
Flo	7	7		8		18	6	4		17	12	12
Emily		0	1		21	21	20	9		11		
Barbara	21	21	21	21			13	21	18	21		
Josie	21	21	6		7	12	4		3		12	7
Lin									4		9	4
Joan	19			16	12	0			15	14	15	15

So in the example below, I have selected the cell B2 because I want to freeze the row above this cell (the dates), and freeze the column to the left of the cell (the names), as you can see in the screen print below.

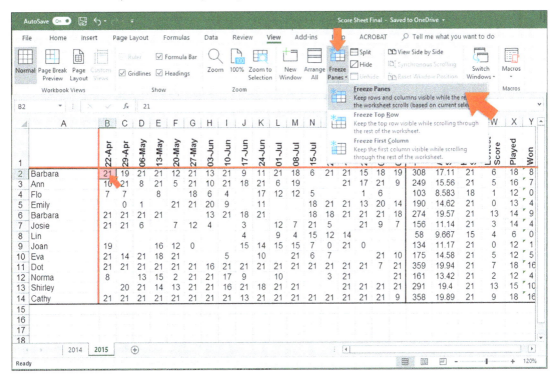

Once you have selected the cell. From your view ribbon, click 'freeze panes' then from the drop down menu click 'freeze panes'.

Split Screen

This is particularly useful if you have a large spreadsheet where you need to see two different parts at the same time.

To split your screen vertically, select a cell in the top row where you want the screen to split. Go to your 'view' ribbon tab and select 'split'. A divider will appear.

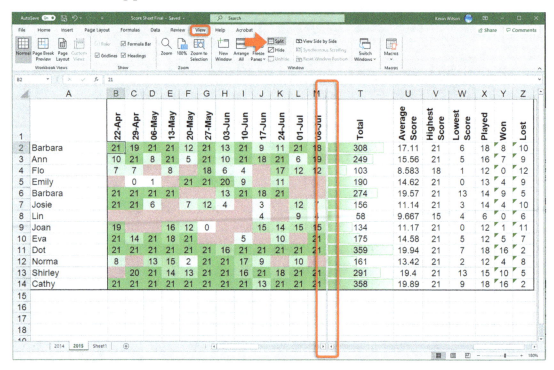

To split your screen horizontally, select a cell in the first column where you want the screen to split. Go to your 'view' ribbon tab and select 'split'. A divider will appear.

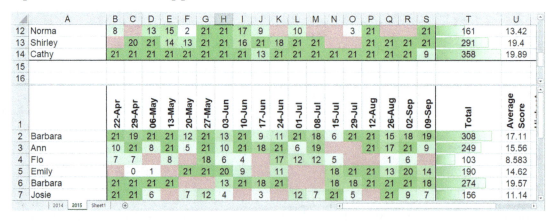

You can click and drag the divider to resize the split.

Importing Data from a CSV File

You can import data from difference sources. This could be a list of names and addresses or a bank statement data you can download from your Bank. Make sure you download your data as comma separated, either a TXT file or CSV file.

You can import the data using Excel's import wizard. As an example, I have included some test data from a sample bank statement for you to practice with.

You can download the test data file **statement test data.csv** from

```
elluminetpress.com/excel
```

To import the data, open a new spreadsheet and from the data ribbon, click 'From Text/CSV'.

In the dialog box that appears, select your data file. In this example **statement test data.csv**.

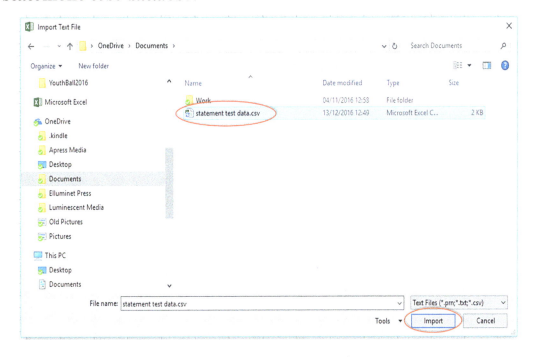

When you have done that, click import.

Now you have to tell Excel how your data is 'delimited' or separated from each other. To show you what this means, if we open the file in notepad, you can see we have a list of transactions. The data in each transaction in the list is separated or 'delimited' with a comma: Date, Account Number, Amount, Sub Category, Description.

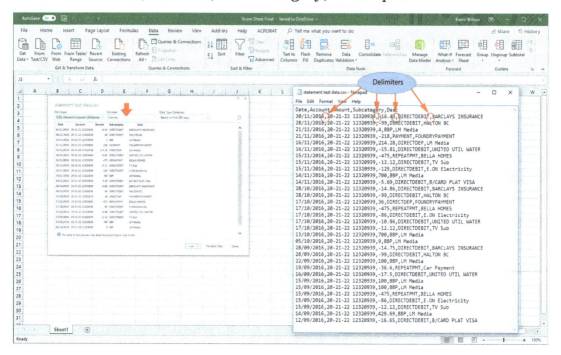

So in the dialog box, select 'delimited' and click next.

The data is separated, or delimited by a comma. So in the 'delimiter' drop down menu, select 'comma'.

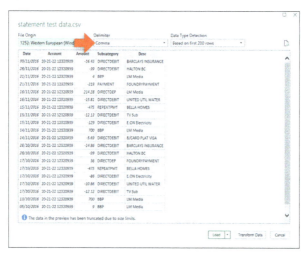

Notice the data in the preview has now been separated into Excel columns. Click 'load'. The data will appear as a new worksheet.

Importing Data from Other Sources

You can import data from a variety of different sources. You'll see the options in the 'get & transform data' section of the 'data' ribbon tab.

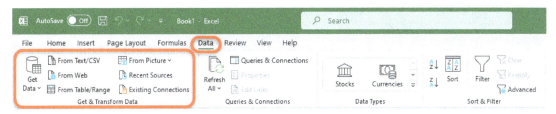

From Picture allows you to extract data from a picture or image and convert it into a table or editable text. This feature is particularly useful when you have printed or handwritten documents that you want to digitize.

From the 'Data' tab, select 'Get Data' and choose 'From Picture'. Then select 'picture from file'.

Browse for the file (eg tabledata.png) on your computer, select it, then click 'insert'.

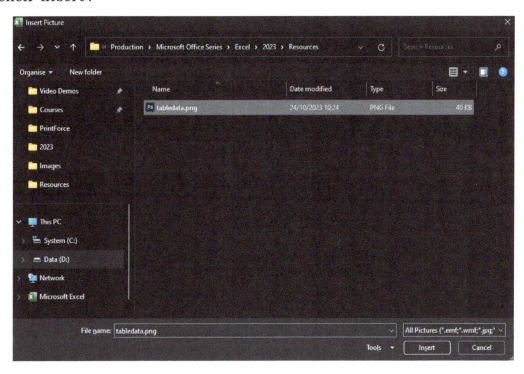

Excel will use Optical Character Recognition (OCR) technology to analyze the image and convert it into text.

This might take a few minutes.

Once the image has been analysed, review and edit the extracted text as needed to ensure accuracy. Click on any of the cells to edit the data. You'll also notice some cells highlighted in red. This means Excel struggled to extract the data and might not have done it accurately.

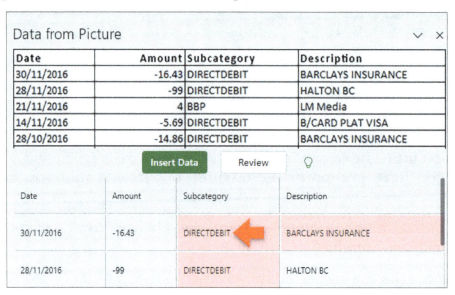

Click 'insert data' when you're done.

From Web allows you to import data directly from web pages or web services. You can extract tables, lists, and other structured data from websites and use it in your Excel workbook.

From the 'Data' tab, select 'Get Data' then choose 'From Web'. Enter the URL of the web page containing the data you want to import. For example:

```
elluminetpress.com/2023/10/what-is-windows-11s
```

Click 'connect' if prompted.

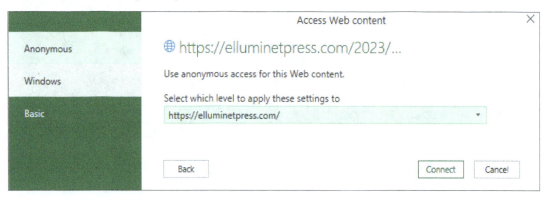

Excel will scape the webpage.

Use the navigator to select specific elements or tables to import. Listed down the left hand panel, you'll see the tables that Excel has extracted. Select the table, click 'load'.

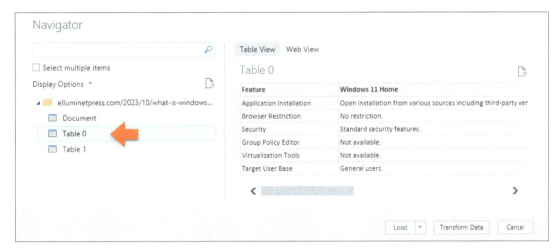

From Database provides various options for importing data from databases, including Microsoft SQL Server, Microsoft Access, MySQL, and Oracle. You can establish database connections and import tables, views, or query results.

From the 'Data' tab, select 'Get Data' and choose the database source you want to connect to. For example 'microsoft access database'.

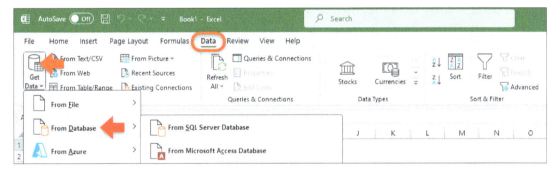

If you're connecting to a database server such as MySQL, provide any connection details such as server name and credentials when prompted.

From the 'navigator', select the tables, or queries you want to import.

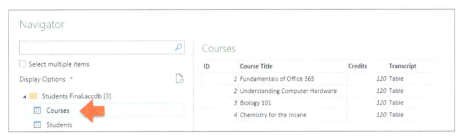

Conditional Formatting

Conditional formatting allows you to change the format of a cell depending on the cell's contents or value. For example, in our score sheet, I want to highlight all the wins for each player. In this particular sport a score of 21 is a win, so we can apply some conditional formatting to change the color of each cell with the number 21.

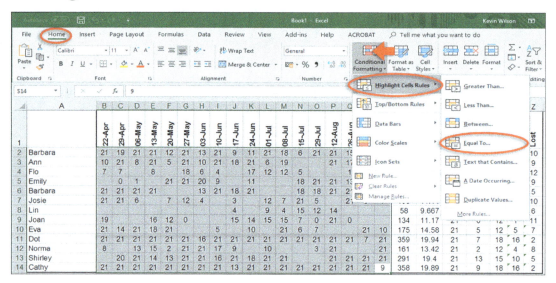

First, highlight the range of cells you want to apply the conditional formatting to. In this example, it's the range B2 to S14 - all the player's scores.

Next, from your home ribbon, click 'conditional formatting'. You'll see a drop down menu with some options. We want to highlight the cells that have a score of 21, so in the menu, go to 'highlight cell rules'. From the slide out, you can select your conditions. In this example, we're highlighting cells with a value equal to 21, so click 'equal to...'

In the 'equal to' dialog box, enter the number your cells must be equal to, in this example, '21'. In the drop down box, select a format. Green is usually good to indicate positives like a win, so select 'green fill with dark green text'. Click OK when you're done.

Taking it a step further, you can also apply different pre-set effects to the cells according to their value. For example, in our scoring sheet, you could have a different shade for each value. 21 being the highest score and a win could be dark green, and each value below 21 could have a lighter shade as the number decreases. So you end up with a very light green at the lowest scores.

You can do this with color scales. From your home ribbon, click 'conditional formatting', select 'color scales', then from the slide out menu, select a style. I'm going to go for the bottom left option with a dark to green color scale.

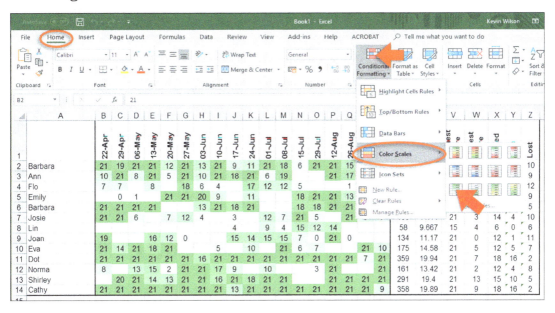

Any blank cells in the table are when a player was either absent or didn't play. We could highlight these in light red. For this one, select 'conditional formatting' from your home ribbon, go to 'highlight cell rules' and from the slide out menu, click 'more rules'.

From the dialog box, in the 'select a rule type' section, select 'format only cells that contain', because we are formatting according to a specific value or condition (ie blank cells).

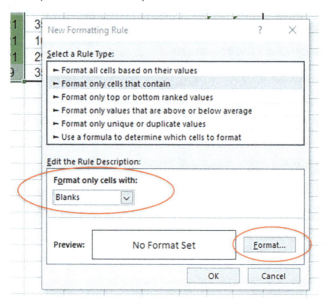

Then in the 'edit the rule description' section, change this to 'blanks' because we are checking for blank cells.

Next click 'format', then select a color to shade the cell when Excel finds a blank. In this example, I'm choosing a light red.

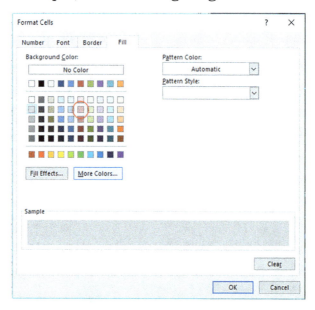

Click 'ok' on both dialog boxes.

For the totals column you could add data bars. You'll need to widen the totals column a bit to see the effect.

Select the total column.

	22-Apr	29-Apr	06-May	13-May	20-May	27-May	03-Jun	10-Jun	17-Jun	24-Jun	01-Jul	08-Jul	15-Jul	29-Jul	12-Aug	26-Aug	02-Sep	09-Sep	Total	Average Score	Highest Score	Lowest Score	Played	Won	Lost
Barbara	21	19	21	21	12	21	13	21	9	11	21	18	6	21	21	15	18	19	308	17.11	21	6	18	8	10
Ann	10	21	8	21	5	21	10	21	18	21	6	19			21	17	21	9	249	13.56	21	5	16	7	9
Flo	7	7		8		18	6	4		17	12	12	5			1	6		103	8.583	18	1	12	0	12
Emily		0	1		21	21	20	9		11			18	21	21	13	20	14	190	14.62	21	0	13	4	9
Barbara	21	21	21	21			13	21	18	21			18	18	21	21	21	18	274	19.57	21	13	14	9	5
Josie	21	21	6		7	12	4		3		12	7	21	5		21	9	7	156	11.14	21	3	14	4	10
Lin								4		9	4	15	12	14					58	9.667	15	4	6	0	6
Joan	19			16	12	0		15	14	15	15	7	0	21	0				134	11.17	21	0	12	1	11
Eva	21	14	21	18	21		5		10		21	6	7			21	10		175	14.58	21	5	12	5	7
Dot	21	21	21	21	21	21	16	21	21	21	21	21	21	21	21	7		21	359	19.94	21	7	18	16	2
Norma	8		13	15	2	21	21	17	9		10			3	21			21	161	13.42	21	2	12	4	8
Shirley		20	21	14	13	21	21	16	21	18	21	21			21	21	21	21	291	19.4	21	13	15	10	5
Cathy	21	21	21	21	21	21	21	13	21	21	21	21	21	21	21	21	21	9	358	19.89	21	9	18	16	2

From your home ribbon click 'conditional formatting'. Go down to 'data bars' and select a gradient fill from the slide out menu.

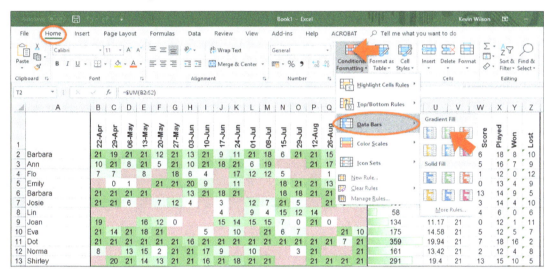

You should end up with something like this. As you can see the higher the final score, the longer the data bar. This is useful for making totals at a glance easier to process.

	22-Apr	29-Apr	06-May	13-May	20-May	27-May	03-Jun	10-Jun	17-Jun	24-Jun	01-Jul	08-Jul	15-Jul	29-Jul	12-Aug	26-Aug	02-Sep	09-Sep	Total
Barbara	21	19	21	21	12	21	13	21	9	11	21	18	6	21	21	15	18	19	308
Ann	10	21	8	21	5	21	10	21	18	21	6	19			21	17	21	9	249
Flo	7	7		8		18	6	4		17	12	12	5			1	6		103
Emily		0	1		21	21	20	9		11			18	21	21	13	20	14	190
Barbara	21	21	21	21			13	21	18	21			18	18	21	21	21	18	274
Josie	21	21	6		7	12	4		3		12	7	21	5		21	9	7	156
Lin								4		9	4	15	12	14					58
Joan	19			16	12	0		15	14	15	15	7	0	21	0				134
Eva	21	14	21	18	21		5		10		21	6	7			21	10		175
Dot	21	21	21	21	21	21	16	21	21	21	21	21	21	21	21	7		21	359
Norma	8		13	15	2	21	21	17	9		10			3	21			21	161
Shirley		20	21	14	13	21	21	16	21	18	21	21			21	21	21	21	291
Cathy	21	21	21	21	21	21	21	13	21	21	21	21	21	21	21	21	21	9	358

Using Multiple Workbooks

If you have multiple workbooks open at a time, you can easily switch between them on Windows 10. To do this, click the Word icon, on your taskbar.

The workbooks that are currently open will show up as thumbnails. Just click one of the thumbnails to switch to that document.

You can also display the workbooks side by side. Go to your view ribbon and click 'side by side'

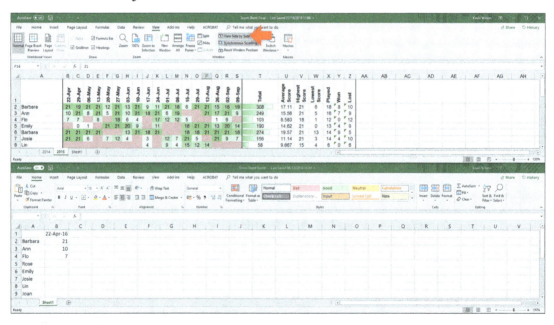

Turn off the synchronous scrolling, otherwise both sheets will scroll at the same time, although this feature can be useful if you are comparing two workbooks.

You can also arrange the windows vertically if that's easier to read. Go to your view ribbon, click 'arrange all'.

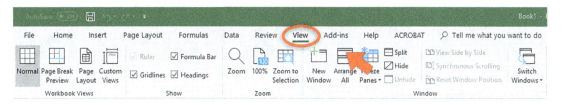

From the pop up dialog box select 'vertical'.

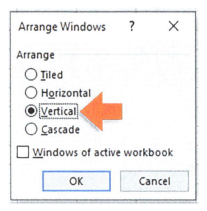

All files open in Excel will be arranged on your screen according to the setting you chose. In this case the two open windows are arranged vertically.

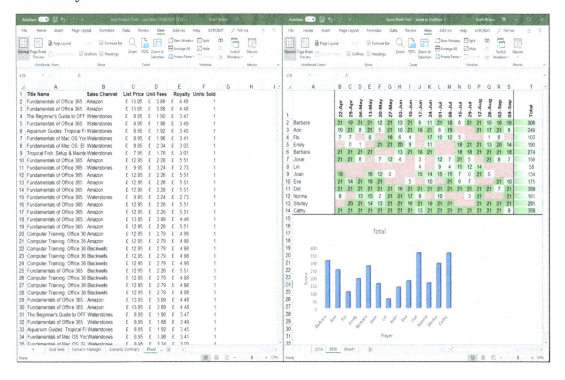

Functions & Formulas

Excel functions and formulas are at the core of what makes Microsoft Excel such a powerful tool for data analysis, calculations, and automation.

Functions are predefined built-in operations that perform specific tasks or calculations. Formulas are combinations of functions, operators, and cell references that enable you to manipulate data, perform calculations, and generate results.

To help you better understand this section, take a look at the video resources. Open your web browser and navigate to the following website:

elluminetpress.com/exc-func

You'll also need to download the source files from:

elluminetpress.com/excel

Using Formulas

If I wanted to add up all the scores in my score sheet, I could add another column called total and enter a formula to add up the scores for the two weeks the player has played.

To do this, I need to find the cell references for Barbara's scores.

Her scores are in row 2 and columns B and C circled below.

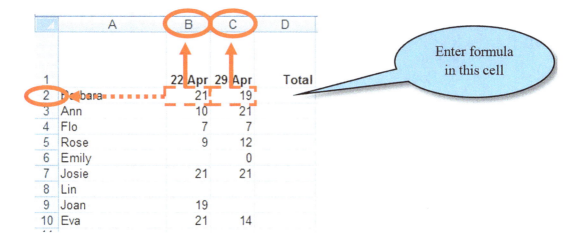

So the cell references are B2 for her score of 21, and C2 for her score of 19.

So we enter into the cell under the heading 'total'

    = B2+C2

Remember all formulas must start with an equals sign (=).

To save you entering the formula for each row, you can replicate it instead.

If you click on the cell D2, where you entered the formula above, you will notice on the bottom right of the box, a small square handle.

I've enlarged the image so you can see it clearly.

Drag this handle down the rest of the column. You can also double click this handle to fill the rest of the column automatically.

| D2 | ▾ ⋮ | ✕ ✓ f_x | =C2+B2 |

◢	A	B 22-Apr	C 29-Apr	D Total
1				
2	Barbara	21	19	
3	Ann	10	21	
4	Flo	7	7	
5	Rose	9	12	
6	Emily		0	
7	Josie	21	21	
8	Lin			
9	Joan	19		
10	Eva	21	14	
11				

Excel will automatically copy the formula and calculate the rest of the totals for you, without you having to enter the formulas for each row.

BIDMAS Rule

BIDMAS (sometimes BODMAS) is an acronym commonly used to remember mathematical operator priority.

Brackets ( )
Indices (square roots: $\sqrt{}$, exponents: squared^2 or cubed^3)
Divide /
Multiply *
Add +
Subtract -

For example, if you wanted to add 20% sales tax to a price of £12.95, you could do something like this...

$$Total = 12.95 + 12.95 * \frac{20}{100}$$

Do the bit circled in red first [multiply & divide], then the addition.

Operators

Excel operators are symbols or characters used to perform various mathematical and logical operations within Excel formulas and functions.

Operators enable you to manipulate and calculate data, make comparisons, and control the flow of your calculations. Excel supports a wide range of operators, including arithmetic, comparison, text concatenation, and logical operators.

Lets take a look at the different types you might find in Excel.

Arithmetic

Arithmetic operators allow you to perform basic mathematical operations such as addition, subtraction, multiplication, division, exponentiation, and modulus (remainder) calculations

Operator	Description	Example	Result
+	Addition	=5 + 3	8
-	Subtraction	=8 - 2	6
*	Multiplication	=4 * 5	20
/	Division	=10 / 2	5
^	Exponentiation	=2^3	8
%	Modulus (remainder)	=10 % 3	1

Comparison

Comparison operators enable you to compare values in Excel. They are used to check if values are equal, not equal, greater than, less than, greater than or equal to, or less than or equal to each other.

Operator	Description	Example	Result
=	Equal To	=A1 = B1	TRUE
<>	Not Equal To	=A1 <> B1	FALSE
>	Greater Than	=A1 > B1	TRUE
<	Less Than	=A1 < B1	FALSE
>=	Greater Than or Equal To	=A1 >= B1	TRUE
<=	Less Than or Equal To	=A1 <= B1	FALSE

Text Concatenation

The text concatenation operator allows you to combine or concatenate text strings in Excel. It's used to join text values or cell contents into a single text string.

Operator	Description	Example	Result
&	Concatenation	="Hello" & " " & "World"	"Hello World"

Logical

Logical operators in Excel are used for evaluating logical conditions. They allow you to perform logical AND, OR, and NOT operations to make decisions based on multiple conditions.

Operator	Description	Example	Result
AND	Logical AND	=AND(A1 > 10, B1 < 20)	TRUE
OR	Logical OR	=OR(A1 = "Yes", B1 = "Yes")	FALSE
NOT	Logical NOT	=NOT(A1 = "Done")	TRUE

Reference

Reference operators in Excel are used to specify ranges and separate arguments in functions. They are essential for referring to cells, creating ranges, and passing multiple arguments to functions.

Operator	Description	Example	Result
:	Range Operator	=SUM(A1:A5)	Sum of values in A1 through A5
,	Argument Separator	=AVERAGE(A1, A2, A3)	Average of values in A1, A2, and A3
(space)	Intersection Operator	=SUM(A1:A10 B1:B10)	Sum of values where both ranges intersect

Wildcard

Wildcard operators are used in text functions to represent variable characters within a text string. They are useful when performing functions like COUNTIF.

Operator	Description	Example	Result
*	Asterisk (used with text functions)	=COUNTIF(A1:A10, "App*")	Counts cells with text starting with "App"

Using Functions

A function is a pre-defined formula. Excel has hundreds of different functions all designed to make analysing your data easier. You can find most of these functions on the formulas ribbon.

The functions are sorted into groups in the 'function library' section. Just click on these to view the list of functions.

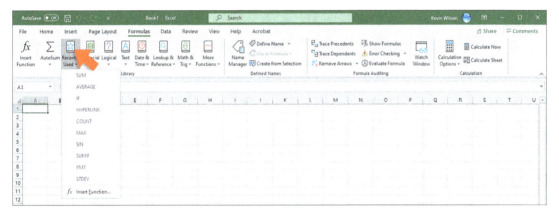

To insert a function into a cell, use the formula bar just under the ribbon menu. So, if I wanted to add a function to cell A1, select A1, then either type the function into the text field or click the 'fx' icon.

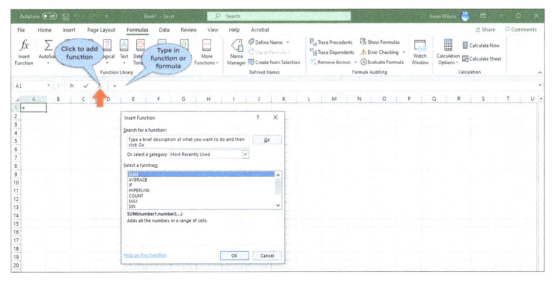

If you click the 'fx' icon, select your function from the dialog box.

Count

Say I wanted to count the number of games played automatically. I could do this with a function.

Insert a new column after "29 Apr" into the spreadsheet and call it "Played". To do this, right click on the D column (the 'Total' column) and from the menu click insert.

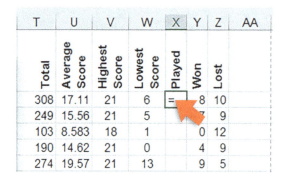

Make sure you have selected the cell you want the formula to appear in, then click 'insert function' (*fx*).

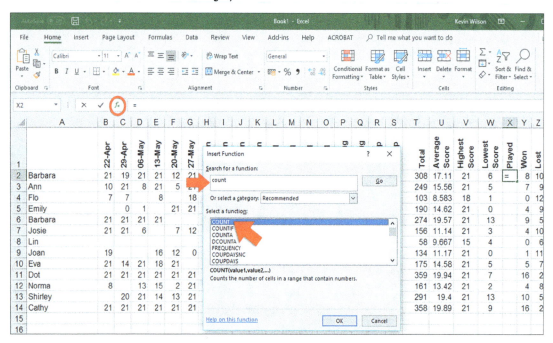

In the insert function dialog box, select the count function from the list then click OK. Type it into the 'search for a function' field if it isn't listed.

Now we need to tell the count function what we want it to count. We want to count the number of games played.

Barbara's scores are in cells B2:S2, so highlight these by dragging your mouse over them, as shown below

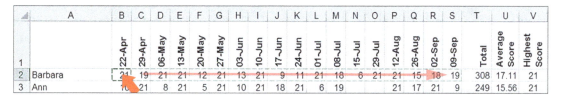

	A	B	C	D	E	F	G	H	I	J	K	L	M	N	O	P	Q	R	S	T	U	V
		22-Apr	29-Apr	06-May	13-May	20-May	27-May	03-Jun	10-Jun	17-Jun	24-Jun	01-Jul	08-Jul	15-Jul	29-Jul	12-Aug	26-Aug	02-Sep	09-Sep	Total	Average Score	Highest Score
1																						
2	Barbara	21	19	21	21	12	21	13	21	9	11	21	18	6	21	21	15	18	19	308	17.11	21
3	Ann	10	21	8	21	5	21	10	21	18	21	6	19			21	17	21	9	249	15.56	21

Click OK in the dialog box.

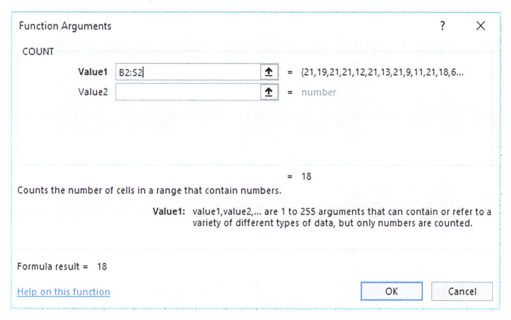

You can see she has played 18 games. Now we can replicate the formula as we did before. Click and drag the small square handle on the bottom right hand side of the cell.

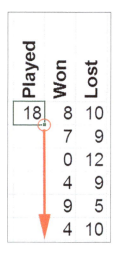

Drag it down to fill the rest of the column.

CountIf

Counting the number of wins gets a little bit more tricky. In this particular sport, a win is the first to 21 points. So we can count the '21s' in the players' scores.

To do this, we use the 'CountIf' function. This function counts a value depending on a certain condition, in this case if the value is 21 or not.

I have inserted another column called 'won'. Click in the first cell of that column. This is where we want the result to appear.

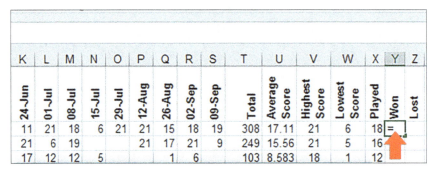

K	L	M	N	O	P	Q	R	S	T	U	V	W	X	Y	Z
24-Jun	01-Jul	08-Jul	15-Jul	29-Jul	12-Aug	26-Aug	02-Sep	09-Sep	Total	Average Score	Highest Score	Lowest Score	Played	Won	Lost
11	21	18	6	21	21	15	18	19	308	17.11	21	6	18	=	
21	6	19			21	17	21	9	249	15.56	21	5	16		
17	12	12	5			1	6		103	8.583	18	1	12		

To insert a CountIf function, click the insert function icon on your ribbon (*fx*).

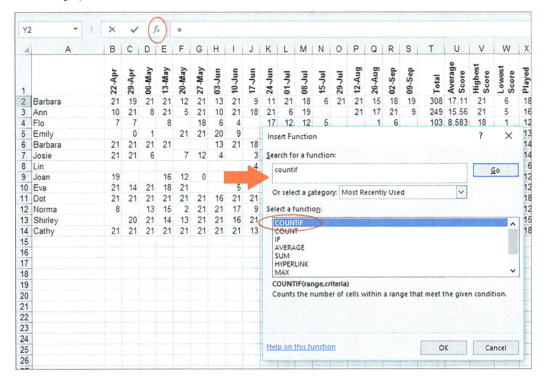

From the dialog box that appears, select 'CountIf'. If it isn't listed, type countif into the search field. Click OK.

Select the range of values you want to count. For Barbara's scores, the range is B2:S2. To do this, click on the cell B2 and drag your mouse over to S2.

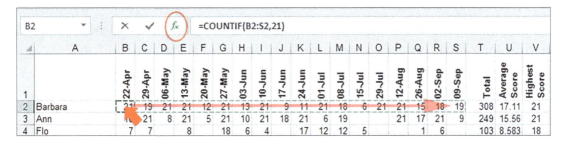

	A	22-Apr	29-Apr	06-May	13-May	20-May	27-May	03-Jun	10-Jun	17-Jun	24-Jun	01-Jul	08-Jul	15-Jul	29-Jul	12-Aug	26-Aug	02-Sep	09-Sep	Total	Average Score	Highest Score
1																						
2	Barbara	21	19	21	21	12	21	13	21	9	11	21	18	6	21	21	15	18	19	308	17.11	21
3	Ann		21	8	21	5	21	10	21	18	21	6	19			21	17	21	9	249	15.56	21
4	Flo	7	7		8		18	6	4		17	12	12	5			1	6		103	8.583	18

In the criteria field enter the number 21, because we want to count the number of '21s' in the range.

Click OK.

Now replicate the function down the rest of the column. Drag the square handle on the bottom right of the cell.

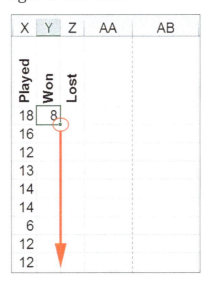

Auto Sum

Auto sum, as its name suggests, adds up all the values in a row or column.

To add up a row, click on the cell you want the total to appear in. In this example, I have created a column for totals, and I want the total for the first player to appear in cell T2, circled below in the illustration.

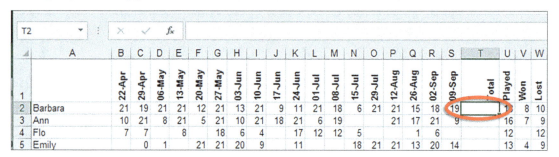

Next, add the auto sum function. You'll find this on your home ribbon. Click on the 'auto sum' icon.

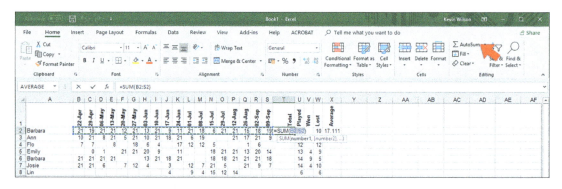

You'll notice, the auto sum function has highlighted the row I want to add up. Press the enter key on your keyboard to execute the function.

Now replicate the function to fill the rest of the column by dragging the handle down, as shown below.

| | E | F | G | H | I | J | K | L | M | N | O | P | Q | R | S | T | U | V | W | X |
	13-May	20-May	27-May	03-Jun	10-Jun	17-Jun	24-Jun	01-Jul	08-Jul	15-Jul	29-Jul	12-Aug	26-Aug	02-Sep	09-Sep	Total	Played	Won	Lost	
2	21	12	21	13	21	9	11	21	18	6	21	21	15	18	19	308	18	8	10	
3	21	5	21	10	21	18	21	6	19			21	17	21	9		16	7	9	
4	8		18	6	4		17	12	12	5			1	6			12		12	
5		21	21	20	9		11			18	21	21	13	20	14		13	4	9	
6	21			13	21	18	21			18	18	21	21	21	18		14	9	5	
7		7	12	4		3		12	7	21	5		21	9	7		14	4	10	
8				4			9	4	15	12	14						6		6	
9	16	12	0		15	14	15	15	7	0	21	0					12	1	11	

Average

Average finds the middle number in a row or column. To find the average, click on the cell you want the result to appear in. In this example, I have inserted a column for average score, and I want the average for the first player to appear in cell U2, circled below left in the illustration.

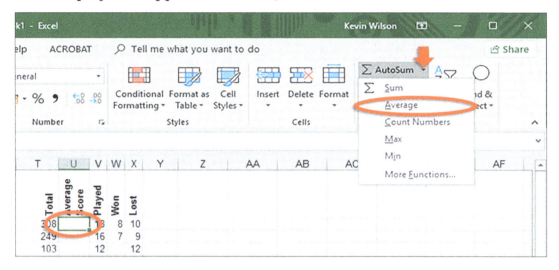

Next, add the average function. You'll find this on your home ribbon. Click on the small down arrow next to the auto sum icon. From the drop down menu, select 'average'. Now, you'll notice that the average function includes the totals column. This is not what we want to average, so you'll need to select the range B2:S2. Click on the cell B2 and drag the box across to S2. Hit return to enter the function.

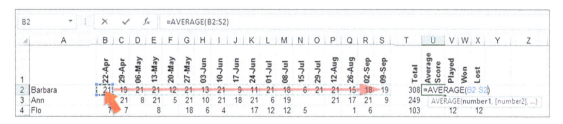

Now replicate the function down the rest of the column.

08-Jul	15-Jul	29-Jul	12-Aug	26-Aug	02-Sep	09-Sep	Total	Average Score	Played	Won	Lost
18	6	21	21	15	18	19	308	17.1	18	8	10
19			21	17	21	9	249	15.6	16	7	9
12	5			1	6		103	8.58	12		12
	18	21	21	13	20	14	190	14.6	13	4	9
	18	18	21	21	21	18	274	19.6	14	9	5
7	21	5		21	9	7	156	11.1	14	4	10

Max & Min

Max returns the largest number in a selected range of values, and min returns the smallest number.

Select the cell you want the result to appear in. I have added two new columns, one for highest score and one for lowest score. I'm going to use the max function in the 'highest score' column.

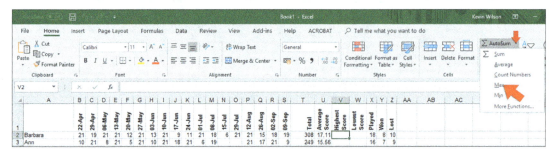

From your home ribbon, click the small down arrow next to the auto sum icon, and from the drop down menu, select 'max'.

Now, you'll notice that the max function has included 'total' and 'average score', this is not what we want. Select the range B2:S2 - click on the cell B2, then drag your mouse pointer over to S2.

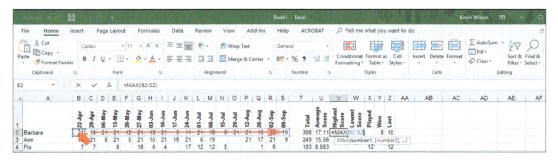

Hit enter to execute the function, then drag the square handle on the bottom right of the cell to replicate the function down the rest of the column.

Total	Average Score	Highest Score	Lowest Score
308	17.1	21	
249	15.6		
103	8.58		
190	14.6		

The procedure is exactly the same for the Min function, except from the auto sum drop down menu select 'min' instead of 'max'. Give it a try.

IF Function

If functions are called conditional functions and test whether a condition is true or false. The function returns a different result for the true condition and another result for false.

```
= (IF condition, result-if-true, result-if-false)
```

Can be read as

```
If test condition is true,
     execute result-if-true
else
     execute result-if-false
```

In the example **IF function demo.xlsx**, we are going to apply a conditional function to calculate our shipping cost. The rule is, free delivery for orders over £25, otherwise a shipping charge of £3.99 applies.

To insert an IF function, click on the cell you want the calculation to appear in (D12).

Then go to your formulas ribbon and click 'insert function'.

From the dialog box that appears, select IF. *If the function isn't in the list, type IF into the search field and click 'go'.*

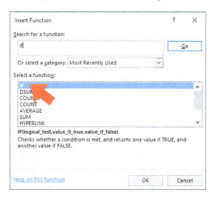

Click OK when you're done.

Chapter 4: Functions & Formulas

Now to build the IF function. First, we need to find out if the total is greater than or equal to 25.

In the function arguments dialog box, click in the 'logical test' field

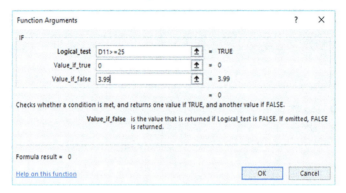

The net total is in cell D11, so click D11 to add this cell to the logical test.

Click back in the logical test field and add the following:

>=25

In the 'value if true' field type 0, because if the net total is over 25, the logical test condition is true, so it's free delivery over £25

In the 'value if false' type 3.99, because if it's under £25 we charge the fee.

Click OK.

Because the net total is £27.46, this is over 25, so the shipping is 0.

Try adjusting the number of items and see what happens when the total goes below £25.

VLookup

VLOOKUP searches for a value in the first column of a specified table, and returns a value from the specified adjacent column.

```
=VLOOKUP (value to look for,
         table to retrieve value from,
                column number with value to return,
                   true for exact/false for approx)
```

In the example **VLOOKUP function demo.xlsx**, we are going to apply a lookup function to calculate our shipping cost according to the shipping rates table (F15:G20).

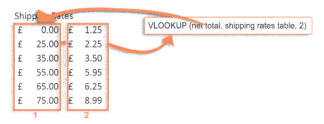

To insert a VLOOKUP, click on the cell you want the calculation to appear in (D12), then go to your formulas ribbon and click 'insert function'.

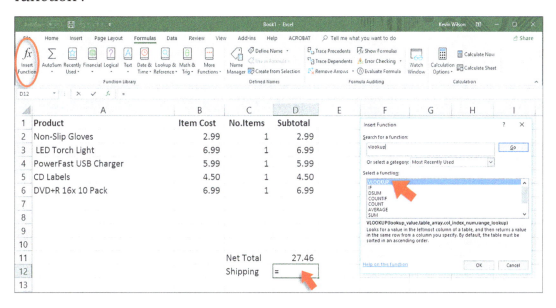

From the dialog box that appears, select VLOOKUP.

If the function isn't in the list, type VLOOKUP into the search field and click 'go'.

Click OK when you're done.

Chapter 4: Functions & Formulas

In the 'function arguments' dialog box, click in the first argument box, 'lookup value'. This is the value we want to look up in the shipping rates table. In this case the net total is in cell D11, so click D11 to add the cell to the 'lookup value' field.

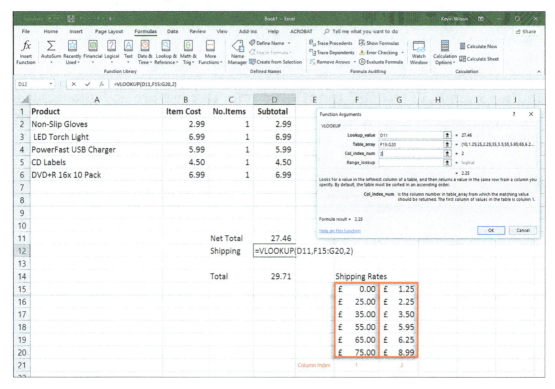

Next click in the 'table array' field. In this field, we want to specify the table of values we are looking up. In this case the table array is the shipping rates table (highlighted in red, above). So click on F15 and drag your mouse over to G20, to select the table.

Now click in the 'col index num' field. This is the column in the table that contains the values we want to return.

So for example, looking at the shipping rates table, if the net total is under 25, we return 1.25.

If the net total is between 25 and 34, we return 2.25 and so on.

The net total range is column 1 and the shipping rates are column 2. We want to return the shipping rates, so type 2 in the 'col index num' field.

Click OK.

Try adjusting the item prices or number of items and see what happens to the shipping rate.

INDEX and MATCH

The INDEX and MATCH functions in Excel are a dynamic duo that allows you to perform advanced lookup and retrieval operations in your spreadsheets. While VLOOKUP and HLOOKUP are commonly used for lookup tasks, INDEX and MATCH provide more flexibility and power when it comes to finding specific values within large datasets.

The INDEX function is used to retrieve the value from a specific row and column within a range of cells. It's a versatile function that can be employed for various purposes, including data extraction, creating dynamic reports, and building interactive dashboards.

The MATCH function is used to locate the position of a specific item within a range. It's particularly helpful when you need to find the relative position of an item, such as locating a product name in a list.

In one of the cells we can add the formula

=INDEX(E2:E7, MATCH("Emily", B2:B7, 0))

E2:E7 is the range where you want to retrieve the hire dates.

MATCH("Emily", B2:B7, 0) is used to find the row number that contains "Emily."

Excel will return 2018-11-03 as Emily's hire date.

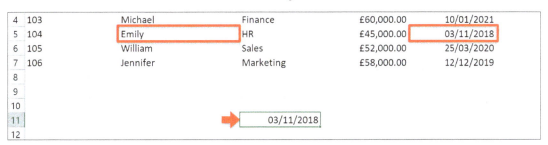

Types of Data & Number Formats

There are several different types of data you will come across while using Excel. These data can be numeric such as whole numbers called integers (eg 10), numbers with decimal points (eg 29.93), currencies (eg £4.67 or $43.76), as well as date and time, text and so on.

Number Format	Description	Example
General	Default format with no specific formatting.	123.45
Number	Standard number format with commas and decimal places.	1,234.56
Currency	Currency format with the currency symbol and commas.	$1,234.56 or £1,234.56
Accounting	Currency format aligned by the currency symbol.	$ 1,234.56 or £ 1,234.56
Percentage	Displays numbers as percentages with a "%" symbol.	12.34%
Date	Date format with various date representations.	10/25/2023 or 25-Oct-23
Time	Time format with hours, minutes, and seconds.	15:30:00
Scientific	Scientific notation with "E" for exponent.	1.23E+03
Fraction	Fraction format showing fractions, e.g., 1/4.	1/4
Text	Display as text, preserving leading zeros.	00123
Custom	User-defined format using custom codes.	$1,234.56 or 12.3 "kg"
Accounting	Accounting format with negative numbers in red.	$ (1,234.56)

Going back to our scoring spreadsheet, we need another column for the average scores. Insert a new column and type the heading 'Average' as shown below.

We are going to work out the average scores over the number of games the players have played. In the Cell F2 enter the formula

```
Average = Total Score / Total number of Games Played
```

The total score is in E2 and the total number of games played is in D2.

So we enter into F2:

```
= E2 / D2
```

Use the forward slash for divide: **/**

Replicate the formula down the column as we did previously in the exercise.

Now the number format isn't as accurate as we want it. We need to tell Excel that the data in this column is a number, accurate to two decimal places. Highlight the cells you want to apply the number format to, as shown below.

	A	B 22-Apr	C 29-Apr	D Played	E Total	F Average
2	Barbara	21	19	2	40	20
3	Ann	10	21	2	31	15.5
4	Flo	7	7	2	14	7
5	Rose	9	12	2	21	10.5
6	Emily		0	1	0	0
7	Josie	21	21	2	42	21
8	Lin			0	0	0
9	Joan	19		1	19	19
10	Eva	21	14	2	35	17.5

On the home ribbon go up to number format (it will currently say 'general' in box). Click the little arrow next to it. From the drop down menu click number. This will format all the selected cells as a number with 2 decimal places.

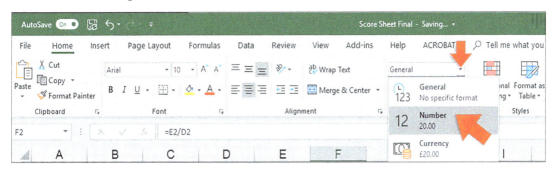

It would be the same for recording the fees paid by the players. Insert another column and call it 'fee'. Say the fees are 4.50. When we enter 4.5 into the cell, Excel thinks it's just a number, so we need to tell Excel that it is currency.

Select all the data in the fee column. You don't need to include the heading row.

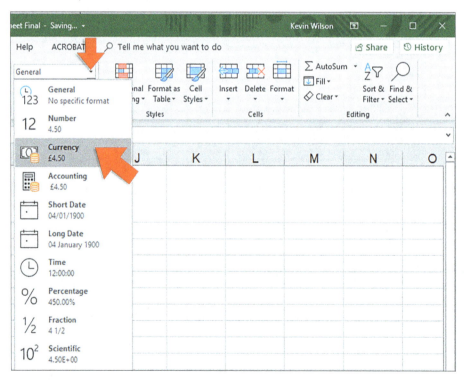

On the home ribbon go up to number format (it will currently say 'general' in box). Click the little arrow next to it.

From the drop down menu click currency. This will format all the numbers as a currency.

Nested Functions

Nested functions allow you to combine multiple functions within a single formula. This capability enables you to create complex calculations and make decisions based on various criteria. By nesting functions, you can build formulas tailored to a specific scenario. These are useful when you need to perform calculations that involve multiple steps or conditions.

Lets say we want to calculate the commission for a sales team based on their monthly sales, but the commission rate depends on their performance tiers.

- If monthly sales are less than $5,000, the commission rate is 2%.
- If monthly sales are between $5,000 and $10,000, the commission rate is 4%.
- If monthly sales are greater than $10,000, the commission rate is 6%.

In the cell C2, you can enter the following nested function:

```
=IF(B2 < 5000, B2 * 0.02, IF(B2 <= 10000, B2 * 0.04, B2 * 0.06))
```

This will calculate the bonus for Salesperson A, as you can see below.

The first IF checks if the sales amount in cell B2 is less than £5,000.

```
IF(B2 < 5000, B2 * 0.02
```

In this case it is, we calculate the commission (B2 * 0.02).

If the sales amount is not less than £5,000, it moves to the second IF.

The second IF checks if the sales amount is less than or equal to £10,000. If it is, it calculates the commission at a rate of 4% (B2 * 0.04).

```
IF(B2 <= 10000, B2 * 0.04, B2 * 0.06)
```

If the sales amount is greater than £10,000, it calculates the commission at a rate of 6% (B2 * 0.06).

Have a look at nestedfunction.xlsx

Text Functions

Text functions in Excel allow you to manipulate and analyze text strings within your spreadsheets. Whether you need to extract specific characters from a cell, combine text from different cells, or format text in a particular way, Excel's text functions provide the flexibility to accomplish these tasks efficiently.

Text Function	Purpose	Syntax	Example
CONCATENATE	Combines multiple text strings into one.	CONCATENATE(text1, [text2], ...)	=CONCATENATE("Hello, ", "World!")
LEFT	Extracts a specified number of characters from the beginning of a text string.	LEFT(text, num_chars)	=LEFT("Excel", 3)
RIGHT	Extracts a specified number of characters from the end of a text string.	RIGHT(text, num_chars)	=RIGHT("Excel", 3)
LEN	Counts the number of characters in a text string.	LEN(text)	=LEN("Microsoft Excel")
FIND	Finds the position of one text string within another.	FIND(find_text, within_text, [start_num])	=FIND("Excel", "Microsoft Excel")
SEARCH	Similar to FIND but not case-sensitive.	SEARCH(find_text, within_text, [start_num])	=SEARCH("excel", "Microsoft Excel")
MID	Extracts a specific number of characters from the middle of a text string.	MID(text, start_num, num_chars)	=MID("OpenAI", 2, 3)
SUBSTITUTE	Replaces occurrences of one text string with another in a text string.	SUBSTITUTE(text, old_text, new_text, [instance_num])	=SUBSTITUTE("apple,banana,apple", "apple", "orange")

For example, suppose you have the following list of names in column A, and we want to extract the first name.

⯅	A	B	C
1	Full Name	First Name	
2	John Smith		
3	Alice Johnsson		
4	David Dames		

In cell B2, where we want the first name to appear, we can enter the following formula to extract the first name from cell A2.

```
=LEFT(A2, FIND(" ", A2) - 1)
```

Here, the function has been used in cell B2.

The FIND function searches for a space (" ") within the text in cell A2 and returns a position. The LEFT function is used to extract characters from the left side of cell A2. The "-1" argument is used to remove the space after first name. Have a look at textfunction.xlsx.

DATE and TIME Functions

Date and time functions in Excel provide tools to work with dates, times, and time intervals in your spreadsheets. Whether you need to calculate durations, format dates, or perform complex date arithmetic, Excel's date and time functions have you covered.

Function	Purpose	Syntax	Example
TODAY	Returns the current date.	TODAY()	=TODAY() returns the current date.
NOW	Returns the current date and time.	NOW()	=NOW() returns the current date and time.
DATE	Creates a date value.	DATE(year, month, day)	=DATE(2023, 10, 23) creates October 23, 2023.
TIME	Creates a time value.	TIME(hour, minute, second)	=TIME(14, 30, 0) creates 2:30 PM.
YEAR	Extracts the year from a date.	YEAR(date)	=YEAR(DATE(2023, 10, 23)) returns 2023.
MONTH	Extracts the month from a date.	MONTH(date)	=MONTH(DATE(2023, 10, 23)) returns 10.
DAY	Extracts the day of the month from a date.	DAY(date)	=DAY(DATE(2023, 10, 23)) returns 23.
DATEDIF	Calculates the difference between two dates.	DATEDIF(start_date, end_date, unit)	=DATEDIF(DATE(2000, 1, 1), DATE(2023, 10, 23), "y") returns the number of years between two dates.

For example, if you wanted to add today's date, type the function into a cell.

```
=today()
```

Cell Referencing

In Excel, there are three types of cell referencing to consider when copying formulas to different parts of your spreadsheet. These types determine how the references in the formula adjust when you paste it elsewhere.

Relative

In relative cell referencing, when a formula or function is copied to different locations in your spreadsheet, the cell references in the formula adjust relative to their new position. For example, if you copy a formula one row down and one column to the right, the references in the formula will shift accordingly.

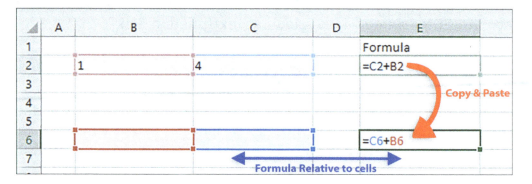

Absolute

Absolute cell referencing means that when you copy a formula or function to other parts of your spreadsheet, the cell references within the formula remain fixed on specific cells, and they do not change. Absolute references are denoted by a dollar sign ($) placed before the column letter, the row number, or both, depending on which part you want to remain constant. In the example below both the column and row are absolute ($H$2) and ($G$2).

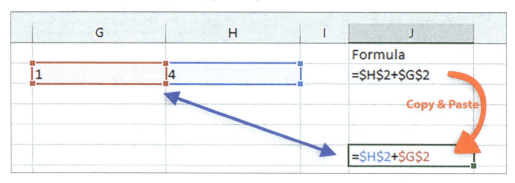

Where you put the dollar sign will indicate which row or column is to remain absolute - meaning it doesn't change when you copy the formula.

$A$1	Column & Row do not change when formula is copied to another cell
A$1	Row does not change, but column will change when formula is copied
$A1	Column does not change, but row will change when formula is copied

Mixed

A mixed cell reference is a combination of both relative and absolute references. It allows you to fix either the row or column while keeping the other part relative. In a mixed reference, the dollar sign ($) is used to lock either the row or column, indicating which part should remain constant when you copy and paste the formula. You can see here in this example that the formula in D2 has B2 as an absolute reference ($B$2), and C2 as a relative reference.

	A	B	C	D
1	Product	Price	Quantity Sold	
2	Product A	10	5	=$B$2*C2
3	Product B	15	3	
4	Product C	12	8	80

Now if we copied the formula, the absolute reference doesn't change, but the relative reference does.

	A	B	C	D
1	Product	Price	Quantity Sold	
2	Product A	10	5	50
3	Product B	15	3	
4	Product C	12	8	=$B$2*C4

Understanding and using these referencing methods is crucial for creating accurate and dynamic calculations, allowing you to work with data effectively across various cells and ensuring that your formulas perform as intended.

In some cases, mixed cell referencing, which combines relative and absolute references, is employed to strike the right balance between adaptability and stability in formulas.

5

Creating Charts

Charts in Microsoft Excel are visual representations of data that allow users to convey complex information in a more understandable and meaningful way. They transform rows and columns of numbers into graphical elements, making it easier to analyze trends, patterns, and relationships within the data.

Whether you're presenting sales figures, tracking project progress, or visualizing survey results, Excel's charting capabilities provide a means to communicate insights, aiding decision-making and enhancing the clarity of reports and presentations.

To help you better understand this section, take a look at the video resources. Open your web browser and navigate to the following website

elluminetpress.com/exc-chart

You'll also need to download the source files from:

elluminetpress.com/excel

Types of Chart

Excel provides a wide range of chart options, such as column, bar, line, pie, and doughnut charts, as well as scatter, bubble, radar, and area charts.

A **Pie Chart** is useful for displaying a category's proportion relative to a whole or total. For example illustrating the distribution of expenses in a budget. Each spending category can be represented as a slice of the pie. This will show which categories consume the largest portions of the budget.

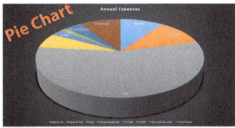

A **Bar Chart** is useful for comparing values across different categories or groups. For example, if you want to display the productivity of employees in a department Each employee's productivity can be represented by a horizontal bar, allowing for a quick visual comparison of who performs best within the team.

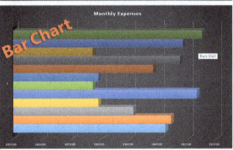

A **Column Chart** is a good choice when you need to compare data across different categories or groups. For example, comparing sales figures for different products over the course of a year. By plotting each product's performance on the vertical axis against the months on the horizontal axis, you can easily identify which products had the highest sales and when those sales peaks occurred.

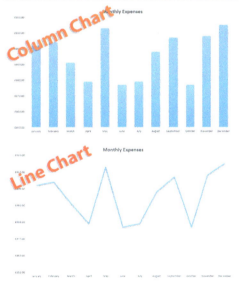

A **Line Chart** is useful when analyzing trends over a period of time. With dates on the x-axis and values you want to analyse (for example temperature) on the y-axis.

Choosing the right chart type enhances the effectiveness of data presentation and analysis. In this chapter, I am going to create a column chart to show the total scores on my scoresheet for each player in the season.

Creating a Chart

First select all the names in the first column. This will be the X-Axis on the chart.

	A	22-Apr	29-Apr	Played	Total	Average	Fee
1		22-Apr	29-Apr	Played	Total	Average	Fee
2	Barbara	21	19	2	40	20.00	£9.00
3	Ann	10	21	2	31	15.50	£9.00
4	Flo	7	7	2	14	7.00	£9.00
5	Rose	9	12	2	21	10.50	£9.00
6	Emily		0	1	0	0.00	£9.00
7	Josie	21	21	2	42	21.00	£9.00
8	Lin			0	0	#DIV/0!	£9.00
9	Joan	19		1	19	19.00	£9.00
10	Eva	21	14	2	35	17.50	£9.00
11							

Now hold down the control key (ctrl) on your keyboard. This allows you to multi-select.

While holding down control, select the data in the total column with your mouse. This will be the Y-Axis on the chart. Note the data in the names column is still highlighted.

E1   fx   Total

	A	22-Apr	29-Apr	Played	Total	Average	Fee
1		22-Apr	29-Apr	Played	Total	Average	Fee
2	Barbara	21	19	2	40	20.00	£9.00
3	Ann	10	21	2	31	15.50	£9.00
4	Flo	7	7	2	14	7.00	£9.00
5	Rose	9	12	2	21	10.50	£9.00
6	Emily		0	1	0	0.00	£9.00
7	Josie	21	21	2	42	21.00	£9.00
8	Lin			0	0	#DIV/0!	£9.00
9	Joan	19		1	19	19.00	£9.00
10	Eva	21	14	2	35	17.50	£9.00

Release the control key and go to the insert ribbon.

In the centre of the ribbon, you will find some different types of charts – line charts, column charts, pie charts.

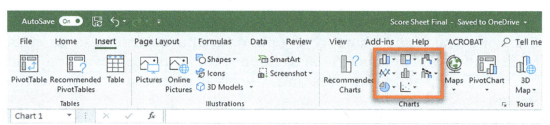

I am going for a nice 3D column chart. Click the 3D column chart shown below to select it.

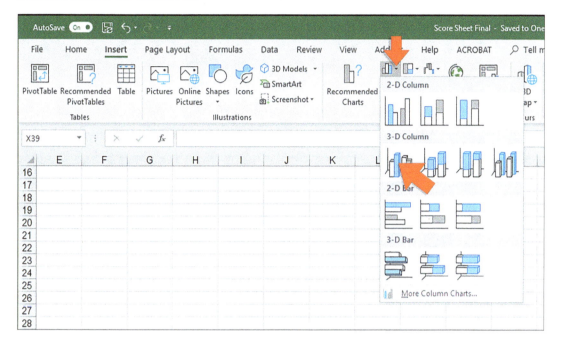

Excel will paste your chart into your spreadsheet.

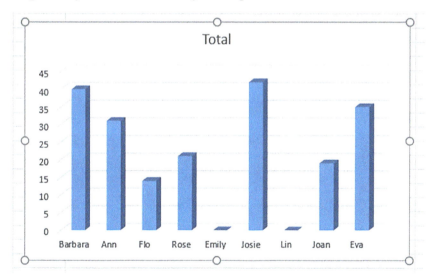

You are automatically taken to the design ribbon where you can select a style to auto-format the chart for you.

Chapter 5: Creating Charts

Select a style from the options that looks good. To see more styles, click the small arrow to the bottom right of the chart styles box.

I'm going for a shaded effect that matches the shading on my table.

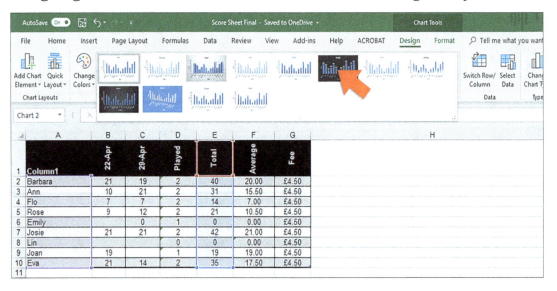

Here, we can see the effect has been added to the chart.

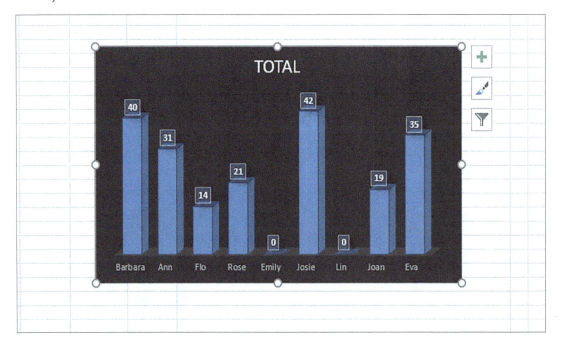

Formatting Charts

You can format and customise the individual chart elements, such as the axis, axis titles, chart title, data labels, gridlines and the legend.

Chart Titles

Excel will automatically give your chart a title, but more often than not, the title isn't very explanatory.

Click on the automatically generated title on your chart, delete the text then type in your own title, 'Final Scores'.

Chart Elements

Charts are made up of elements. These could be axes, titles, gridlines, data and so on. To edit the chart elements, click on your chart to select it.

You'll see three icons appear down the right hand edge of the chart. Click on the top one to reveal the slide out menu. From here, you can add axis titles, chart titles, labels, gridlines and a legend, by clicking the tick boxes next to the elements in the list.

Axis Titles

On some charts, Excel might not have added any axis titles. If this is the case, click your chart then click the chart elements icon, circled below.

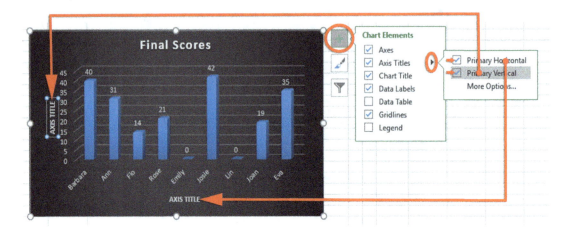

In the slide out menu, click the small right arrow next to 'axis titles'. From the slide out, click both 'primary horizontal' and 'primary vertical', for both X and Y axis on your chart.

To change the text in the axis titles, click on the title, delete the text and type in your titles. In this example, the horizontal axis is 'player name' and the vertical axis is 'final score'.

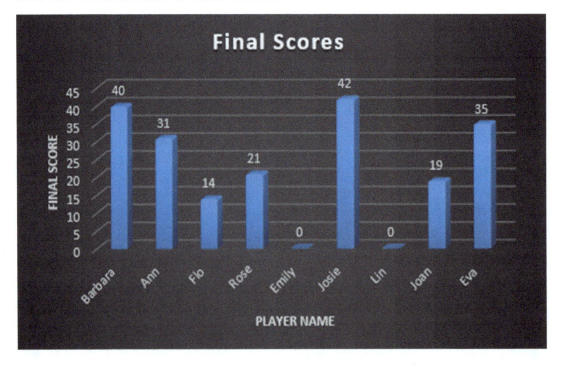

Customising Charts

There are shortcuts to changing elements of your chart, but to give you the most control over the changes, we'll do it this way.

Right click on a blank space on your chart and from the popup menu, click 'format chart area'.

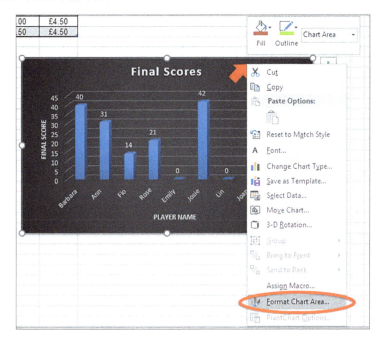

In the side panel that appears, you have a number of options.

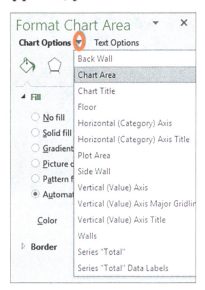

Click the small down arrow next to 'chart options' to open the drop down menu.

Here you can select the element of the chart you want to customise (chart color, labels, and so on).

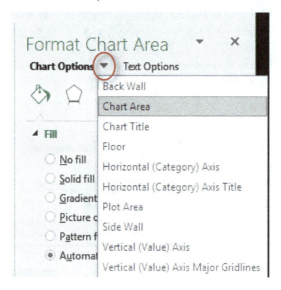

Each option on the menu will change a specific part of your chart. In the illustration below, you can see each part of the chart corresponds to an option on the menu.

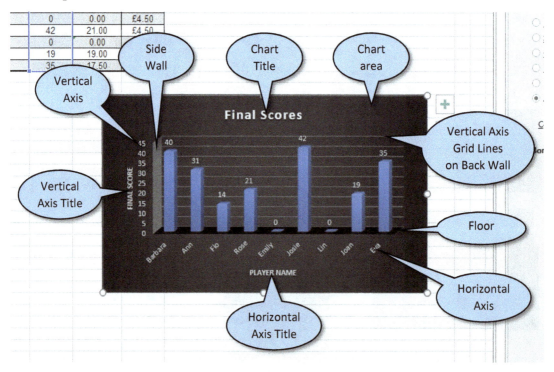

Chart title, horizontal axis, vertical axis, and so on. If you want to change the chart area color, select 'chart area', if you want to change the axis titles, select axis title from the menu, and so on.

Change Background to Solid Color

To change the background color, right click on a blank space on your chart and from the popup menu, click 'format chart area'.

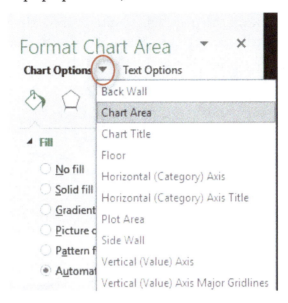

In this example, we want to change the background color. The background is called the 'chart area', so make sure 'chart area' is selected.

To change to a solid color, expand the fill section by clicking on the small down arrow next to fill. Click 'solid fill', then click the down arrow next to the paint pot, and select a color.

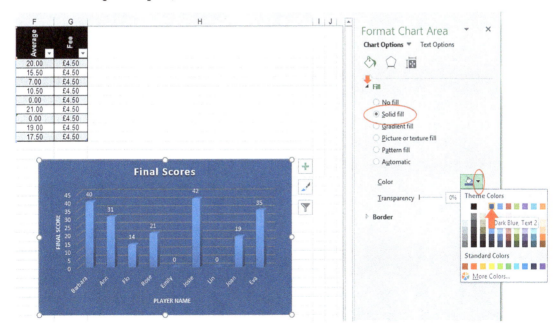

Change Background to Gradient Color

You can also apply a gradient color, meaning one color blends into another over the surface of your chart.

To do this, right click on your chart, click 'format chart'. From the chart options make sure 'chart area' is selected as in the previous section, except from the fill options, click 'gradient fill'.

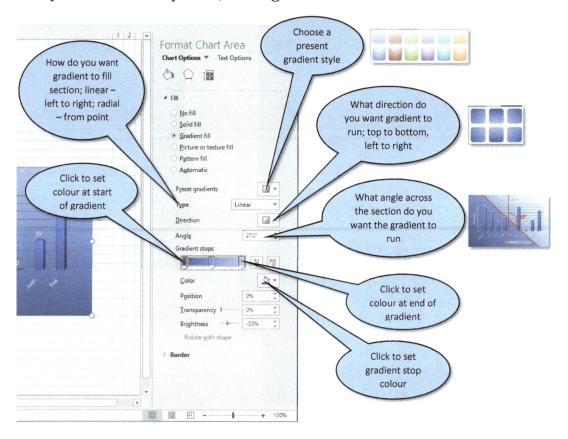

You can customise your gradient. Take a closer look at the bottom section of the gradient settings. You can choose from several gradient presets. Linear gradients run left to right or top to bottom. Radial gradients radiate out from a point on the chart.

You can select the type of gradient from the 'type' drop down field.

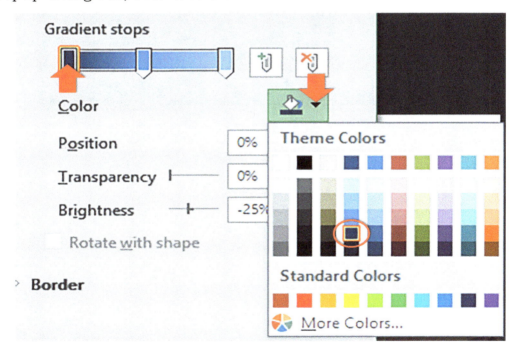

You can also set the angle at which the gradient runs. This only applies to linear gradients and sets the angle at which the color begins to change. As you can see in the example above, the angle is set to 130° which means 130° from the vertical axis shown in red.

Each stop on the gradient bar represents a color. You can change these colors by clicking on the stop, then selecting the paint pot. From the popup dialog box, click a color.

For each of the stops, you can change the position of the gradient (where the color blends), as well as the brightness and transparency of the color gradient.

Change Chart Type

To change your chart type, eg from a column chart to a bar chart, click on your chart and select the design ribbon. From the design ribbon, click 'change chart type'.

From the popup dialog box, look down the left hand side for the types of chart you want (pie, bar, line, etc), and select one.

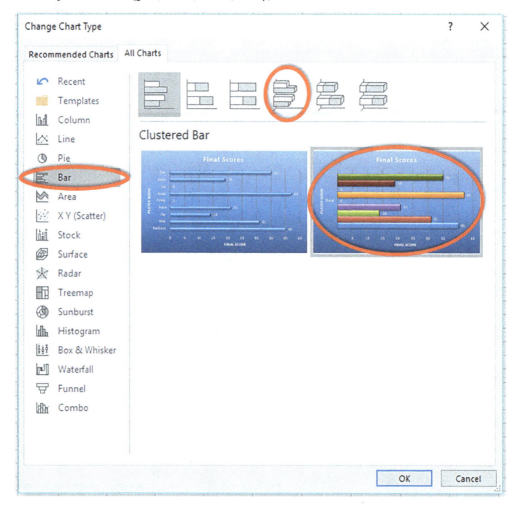

From the right hand pane, select the style of chart you want.

For this example, I am going to choose a nice colorful bar chart.

Move and Resize Charts

To resize, click on a blank section of your chart. You'll notice some small white dots appear around the chart. These are called resize handles. Drag the resize handles across your page to the size you want the chart.

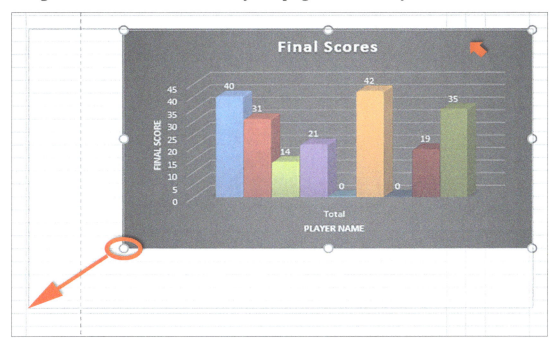

To move your chart into position, click in a blank section of your chart, then drag it with your mouse into a new position.

Edit Chart Data

If you need to change the data in the chart, first click on the chart to select it. When you do this, you'll notice that the data ranges being used for the chart are highlighted. Here in this example, this chart is using column A and Column E.

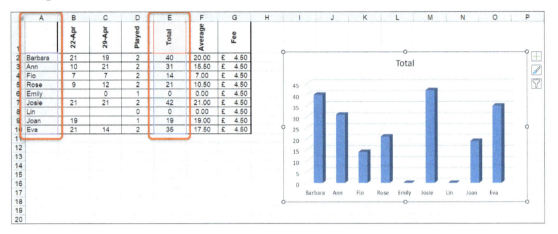

If you want to use a different range of data for the chart, go to the 'chart design' ribbon tab, then click 'select data'.

In the 'Select Data Source' dialog box, you'll see a field labelled 'chart data range'.

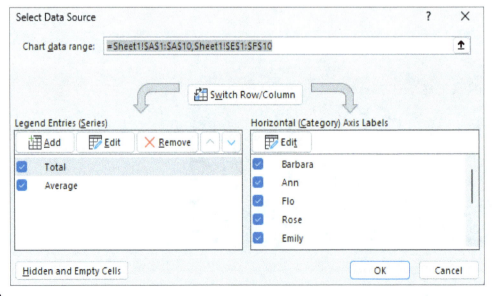

Click and drag to select the new range of cells from the table used to create the chart. If you want to select multiple columns, hold down the control key on the keyboard as you select another row.

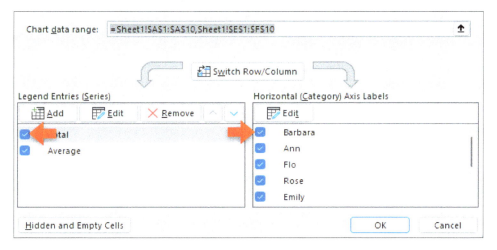

	A	B	C	D	E	F	G	H
		22-Apr	29-Apr	Player	Total	Average	Fee	
1								
2	Barbara	21	19	2	40	20.00	£ 4.50	
3	Ann	10	21	2	31	15.50	£ 4.50	
4	Flo	7	7	2	14	7.00	£ 4.50	
5	Rose	9	12	2	21	10.50	£ 4.50	
6	Emily		0	1	0	0.00	£ 4.50	
7	Josie	21	21	2	42	21.00	£ 4.50	
8	Lin			0	0	0.00	£ 4.50	
9	Joan	19		1	19	19.00	£ 4.50	
10	Eva	21	14	2	35	17.50	£ 4.50	

You can also add or remove axis labels or switch the rows/columns. To do this, check/uncheck labels in the 'legend entries' or 'horizontal axis labels'. To switch the rows/columns around click 'switch row/column'.

Chart data range:	=Sheet1!$A$1:$A$10,Sheet1!$E$1:$F$10	⬆

⟳ 🔲 Switch Row/Column ⟲

Legend Entries (Series)
🔲 Add 📝 Edit ✕ Remove ⌃ ⌄

☑ Total
☑ Average

Horizontal (Category) Axis Labels
📝 Edit

☑ Barbara
☑ Ann
☑ Flo
☑ Rose
☑ Emily

Hidden and Empty Cells   OK   Cancel

After specifying the new range, click 'ok' on the 'Select Data Source' dialog box to apply the changes.

Your chart will update automatically to reflect the new data ranges.

Here in the chart you can see the totals in the blue column, and the average in the red column.

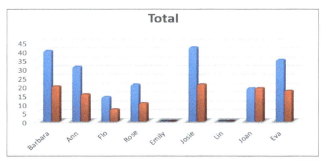

Sparklines

Sparklines are small, simple charts placed in single cells, each representing a series of data in your Excel spreadsheet. They provide a visual representation of data trends over time without specifying numbers or taking up the space that full-sized charts do.

To create a sparkline, first ensure your data is organized in a way that sparklines can interpret, usually in rows or columns.

Go to the 'insert' ribbon tab. In the 'sparklines' group, choose the type of sparkline you want to create. For example select 'line'.

In the 'create sparklines' dialog, for the 'data range' field, click and drag to select the cells B2 to M2.

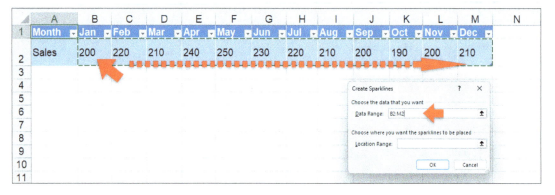

In the 'location range field', click in cell N2. Ensure it says $N$2. This will put the sparkline in cell N2.

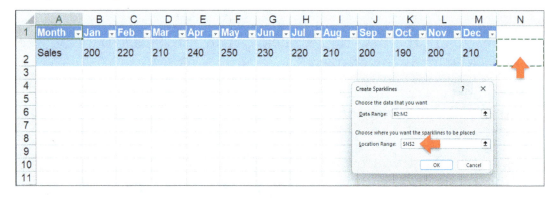

Click 'ok' when you're done.

3D Maps

3D Maps in Excel provide a powerful way to visualize geographical data by plotting it on a three-dimensional globe or custom map. This feature, previously known as Power Map, is particularly useful for interpreting data with geographical elements and generating insights through visual analysis.

Lets say we have some sales data for different cities, and you want to visualize this data on a 3D map. Select the table, go to the 'insert' ribbon tab. Look for the 'tours' group, then click on 3D Map.

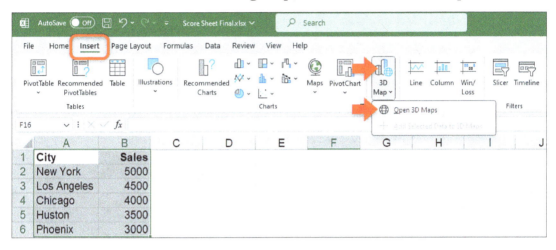

First, add your geographic fields. In the right pane, you will see your data fields listed. Under the 'data' section, click on the 'city' field from the Location box. Select the 'city' field from the drop down menu.

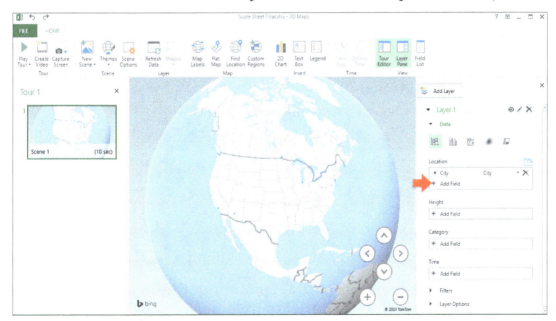

Next, map your date. To do this. Select the 'height' field. Select 'sales' from the drop down menu.

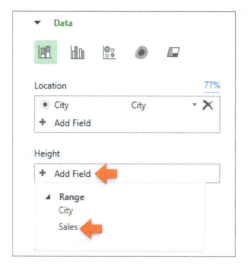

This action will generate bars on the map representing sales figures, with taller bars indicating higher sales.

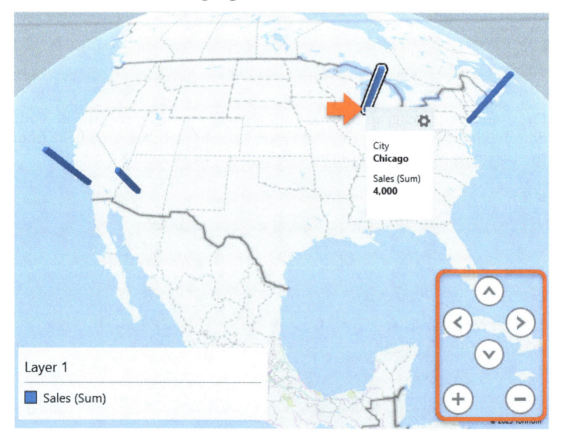

Use the navigation controls on the bottom right to zoom in, zoom out, and rotate the map to view your data from different angles.

Use the 'layer options' section in the Layer Pane on the right hand side to adjust the settings for your map. You can change the color of the bars, adjust the thickness, add data labels, and more to make your map more informative.

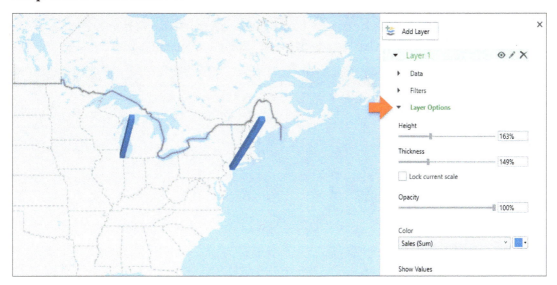

Advanced Charts

Excel provides a variety of advanced chart types that can be used to analyze and visualize data in more complex ways. These charts can be very useful when dealing with multifaceted data or when you need to convey complex information in an understandable manner.

Common Types

Waterfall charts are used to show the cumulative effect of sequential positive and negative values. They are often used for financial statements to show the progressive total when values are added or subtracted.

Histograms are used to group numerical data into bins to show the frequency distribution. They can help to understand the underlying probability distribution of a set.

Funnel charts are often used to represent stages in a process and show values at different stages in a descending manner.

Stock charts are often used to illustrate the movement of stock prices, but they can be used for scientific data as well.

Combo charts combine two or more chart types into a single chart, which is useful when the data types being charted are different scales.

Adding an Advanced Chart

Ensure your data is organized in a table format with a header row. Highlight the range of cells containing your data (A1:C7). Go to the 'insert' ribbon tab, then in the 'charts' group, click on the 'combo' icon. From the dropdown, choose 'clustered column' for the 'sales' series (column) and Line for the 'growth rate' series column.

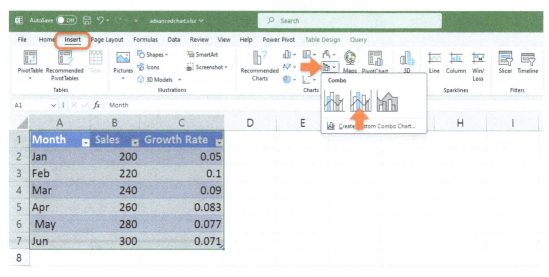

The sales are represented by columns on the primary axis, and the growth rate is represented by a line on the secondary axis, which allows for easy comparison and analysis of the related data series.

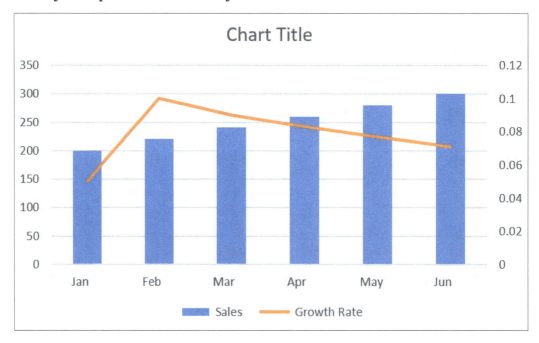

Have a look at advancedcharts.xlsx

Charting Add-Ins

Microsoft Excel's charting functions cover a broad range of needs, however some scenarios call for specialized capabilities. To bridge this gap, several charting add-ins are available that offer additional tools for generating charts.

SmartCharts for Excel is designed that supports a variety of chart types including standard line, bar, pie, and bubble charts, along with trend and multi charts. It uses a simple point and click interface, allowing you to quickly visualize data from any Excel table without needing to do any modelling.

LucidCharts is a diagramming solution that integrates with Excel to create flowcharts, wireframes, and other diagrams. You can create visuals in LucidCharts and embed them directly into Excel spreadsheets.

ChartExpo is a data visualization tool that simplifies the creation of custom charts in Excel. It provides a wide range of advanced Excel charts that allow you to turn complex data into simple, insightful charts or graphs.

PineBI is a charting add-in for Microsoft Excel for creating advanced dynamic charts. With PineBI, you can either create charts based on your own data or add a template which you can then adjust to fit your needs. It's built entirely on native Excel features, allowing you to edit all charts just like the default Excel ones. The add-in allows for the quick transformation of Excel workbooks into dynamic and engaging dashboards. It includes more than 25 widely-used and complex visualizations for data analysis, including Waterfalls, and Actual vs. Target charts among others.

The Visio Data Visualizer add-in for Excel allows you to create high-quality Visio flowcharts, cross-functional flowcharts, and organizational charts directly from your Excel data. It utilizes an online service to generate diagrams.

SmartCharts for Excel is a tool designed for instant analytics and business intelligence within Excel.

It's important to note that some of these add-ins are not a free add-in. Some requires a license after a trial period, and additional purchase may be required.

See "Add-Ins" on page 172 for more information on how to install an Add-In.

6

Data Analysis

Data analysis in Excel is a practice of analysing, transforming and modelling raw data to draw conclusions, and support decision-making.

This could include filtering and sorting the data, or applying various functions and calculations. To aid decision making, charts and tables can be generated to present the data in a meaningful way.

In this chapter, we'll take a look at some common tools used for analysing data such as

- Goal Seek
- Scenario Manager
- Pivot Tables & Charts
- ToolPak & Solver Add-ins

To help you better understand this section, take a look at the video resources. Open your web browser and navigate to the following website:

elluminetpress.com/exc-an

You'll also need to download the source files from:

elluminetpress.com/excel

Introduction

Excel provides a wide range of functions and tools for comprehensive data analysis. You can use formulas, statistical functions, charts, and Pivot Tables for data interpretation and presentation. Tools such as Goal Seek and Scenario Manager further enhance analytical capabilities.

Goal Seek is used to determine the values required to achieve a specific result. It simplifies the process of solving problems by identifying the necessary input needed to meet a predefined target. This is useful when dealing with scenarios where the desired outcome is known, but the input needed to attain it is not.

Scenario Manager is used to create and manage multiple scenarios for data in a worksheet. It allows you to compare different input values and their impact on calculations or outcomes. This tool is particularly useful for exploring various "what-if" scenarios and allows for easy switching between different sets of input values to assess their consequences.

Pivot Tables organize and analyze data. They categorize, count, total, and average data within a table, and give you the flexibility to view data in various ways by rearranging, filtering, or regrouping. This helps you extract insights, identify trends, and make data-driven decisions. Pivot Tables display large datasets in a two-dimensional format using columns, rows, values, and filters.

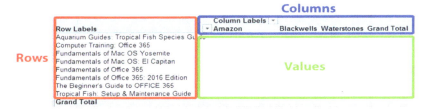

There is also a drill-down function that reveals individual data points behind summarized values and support the integration of calculated fields and items. Slicers let you navigate data within a Pivot Table visually and directly.

A Pivot Chart is a visual representation of the data from a Pivot Table. It provides a graphical way to showcase and analyze the summarized data, making it easier to spot trends, patterns, and outliers.

Goal Seek

Goal seek allows you start with the desired result, the goal in other words, and calculates the value required to give you that result.

For this example, use the **goal seek** worksheet in the **Data Analysis Starter.xlsx** workbook.

Say we want to take out a loan of £10,000. This particular bank has an interest rate of 3.3%. We're paying the loan off over 60 months with a payment of £181.02. We can afford to pay off £200 per month. We can use goal seek to find out how many months we'll be paying the loan off.

First click the monthly payment (cell C4), because this is what we want to change. From the data ribbon, click 'what-if analysis'. From the drop down menu, click 'goal seek'.

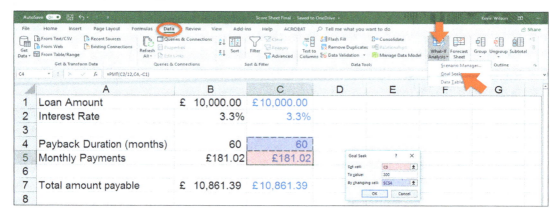

On the dialog box that appears, click in 'to value' and enter 200. This is our target amount or goal.

Now we want to achieve this goal by changing the payback duration, so click in 'by changing cell' on the dialog box, then click the cell with the number of months (C4 in this case).

Click OK. We have an answer... It would take 54 months at £200 a month.

Data Analysis with Scenario Manager

When creating spreadsheets, you will probably want to explore "what-if" scenarios and see how different values effect results. Say we were running a small bookstore. We bought in some books and we want to see what our sales revenue and profit will be for different prices to help us price our books.

For this example, use the **scenario manager** worksheet in the **Data Analysis Starter.xlsx** workbook.

Creating Scenarios

To add a scenario, go to your data ribbon and click 'what-if analysis'. From the drop down menu, select 'scenario manager'.

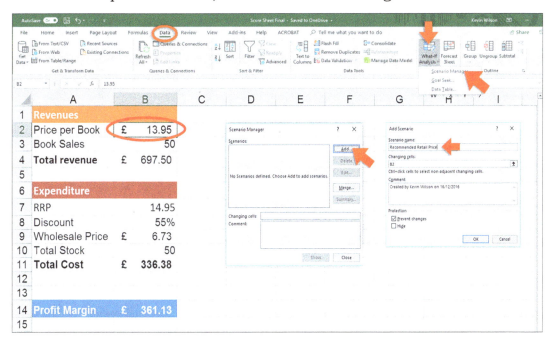

From the dialog box that appears, click add. Then from the 'add scenario' dialog box, type in a meaningful name in the field 'scenario name'.

Click in the 'changing cells' field underneath, then click the cell or cells you want to change. In this case we want to change the price per book in cell B2. So click B2.

Click OK.

Repeat the process and create scenarios for 'Sale Price' at £10.95, and 'Give Away' price at £8.99

Now in the scenario manager dialog box, you'll have three scenarios you can click on, and instantly see the results.

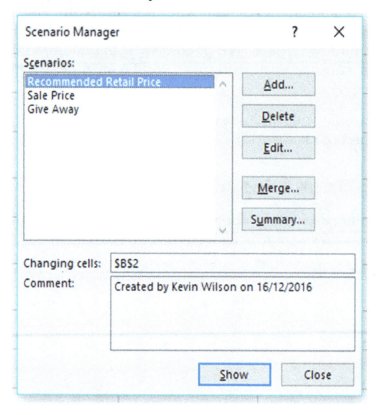

Click on one of the scenarios then click show.

Recommended Retail Price		
Revenues		
Price per Book	£	14.95
Book Sales		50
Total revenue	£	747.50
Expenditure		
RRP		14.95
Discount		55%
Wholesale Price	£	6.73
Total Stock		50
Total Cost	£	336.38
Profit Margin	£	411.13

Sale Price		
Revenues		
Price per Book	£	10.95
Book Sales		50
Total revenue	£	547.50
Expenditure		
RRP		14.95
Discount		55%
Wholesale Price	£	6.73
Total Stock		50
Total Cost	£	336.38
Profit Margin	£	211.13

Give Away Price		
Revenues		
Price per Book	£	8.99
Book Sales		50
Total revenue	£	449.50
Expenditure		
RRP		14.95
Discount		55%
Wholesale Price	£	6.73
Total Stock		50
Total Cost	£	336.38
Profit Margin	£	113.13

If you need to edit any of the scenarios, just click on the name in the scenario list and click edit. You'll be able to go through the add scenario process again and amend the values.

Summary Reports

You can also generate quick reports of your scenarios. To do this, go to your scenario manager.

Data Ribbon -> What-If Analysis -> Scenario Manager

From the scenario manager dialog box, click 'summary'.

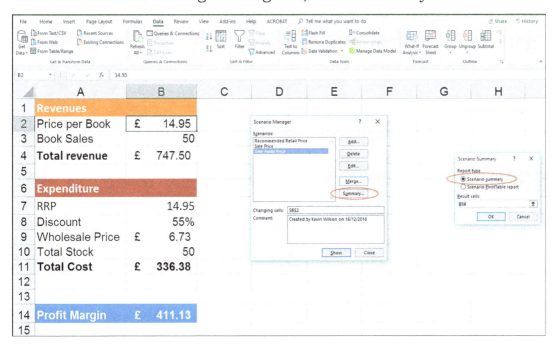

On the scenario summary dialog box, click 'scenario summary', to produce a report.

For the 'result cells', this is the cell or cells we're looking at when we're changing the values in the scenarios.

We want to show how changing the price per book affects profit margin. So here, select B14 because this is where the value for profit margin is.

If we wanted to show how changing the price per book affects total revenue, we'd select the total revenue value in B4.

Click 'ok'.

You'll see a new worksheet appear.

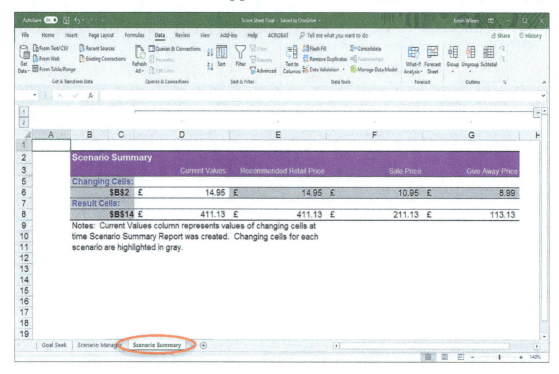

Here you can see Excel has created a new worksheet with our report on. If you look at the report, some labels aren't very clear. In the report, the rows 'changing cells' or 'result cells' don't really tell us much. Good practice is to change these to more meaningful names.

Scenario Summary				
	Current Values:	Recommended Retail Price	Sale Price	Give Away Price
Changing Cells:				
$B$2 £	14.95 £	14.95 £	10.95 £	8.99
Result Cells:				
$B$14 £	411.13 £	411.13 £	211.13 £	113.13

Notes: Current Values column represents values of changing cells at time Scenario Summary Report was created. Changing cells for each scenario are highlighted in gray.

To do this, just delete the text in the cells you want to rename, then type in your own text as shown below.

Scenario Summary				
	Current Values:	Recommended Retail Price	Sale Price	Give Away Price
Scenarios	£	14.95 £	14.95 £	10.95 £	8.99
Profit Margins	£	411.13 £	411.13 £	211.13 £	113.13

Notes: Current Values column represents values of changing cells at time Scenario Summary Report was created. Changing cells for each scenario are highlighted in gray.

This makes a bit more sense.

Creating Pivot Tables

A pivot table is a data summarisation tool and can automatically sort, count, total or average the data stored in one table or worksheet and display the results in a new table or worksheet. Reports can then be produced to present the data. With a pivot table you can quickly pivot data, meaning you reorganise or summarise the data. Pivoting data can help you answer different scenarios, for example, best selling products, sales channels and so on.

For this example, use the **pivot table data** worksheet in the **Data Analysis Starter.xlsx** workbook.

First click in any cell in the data table. This is to indicate to Excel what table of data it should use to create the pivot table. From the 'insert' ribbon, click 'pivot chart'.

Make sure Excel has selected the correct range in the 'select a table or range' field. Excel will indicate the selection with a dashed line around the data. Next, in the dialog box, select 'new worksheet'. Click 'ok'.

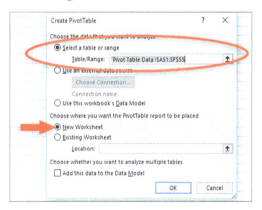

Select and delete the pivot chart, we just want the pivot table at this stage.

You'll see your 'PivotTable Fields' sidebar open on the right hand side.

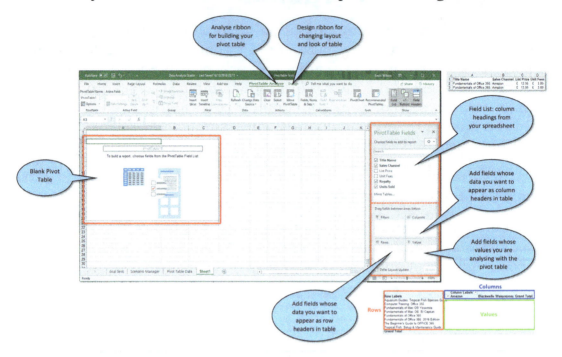

From here we can start building pivot tables. You can add and remove fields. You can drag the fields over to the rows box or the columns box, on the bottom half of the 'PivotTable Fields' sidebar, depending on how you want to analyse your data. Any field you drag to the rows box will appear down the left hand side of the table and anything you drag to the columns box will appear as columns across the top of your table. This makes up the row and column headers of the pivot table.

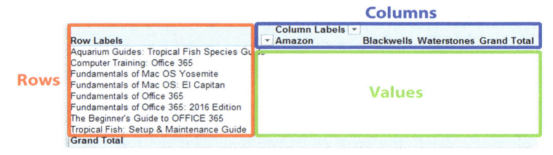

The values box, is the data you want to analyse against the rows and column headers. So, in the example above, our rows are the book titles and the columns are the sales channels.

In the values section, we could add the 'royalty' field to see how much income is generated for each title in each sales channel. Or we could add 'units sold' to the values section to see how many books have sold in each sales channel.

So lets build a pivot table. In this example, we want to find the total income per sales channel.

First add the rows. This will be title name. Either click and drag 'title name' to the 'rows' box, or click the tick next to 'title name'

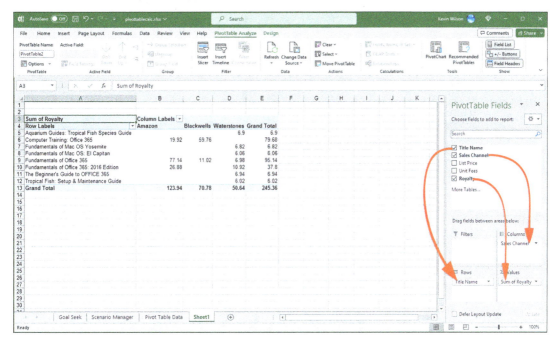

Next we need to add some values. We want the income, in this case income is labelled 'royalty'. So click the tick box next to the 'royalty' field. You can also drag the 'royalty' field over to the 'values' box.

Now we should have a list of books and their total royalties. This is the total income for all sales channels.

Row Labels	Sum of Royalty
Aquarium Guides: Tropical Fish Species Guide	6.9
Computer Training: Office 365	79.68
Fundamentals of Mac OS Yosemite	6.82
Fundamentals of Mac OS: El Capitan	6.06
Fundamentals of Office 365	95.14
Fundamentals of Office 365: 2016 Edition	37.8
The Beginner's Guide to OFFICE 365	6.94
Tropical Fish: Setup & Maintenance Guide	6.02
Grand Total	**245.36**

The next step is to add the sales channels. We want the royalties to be split into columns, one for each sales channel.

So to do this, click and drag the 'sales channel' field over to the 'columns' box.

Now we can see the royalties for each sales channel - Amazon, Blackwells and Waterstones, as well as grand totals. In this case Amazon generated the highest revenue (£123.94).

Sum of Royalty Row Labels	Column Labels ▾ Amazon	Blackwells	Waterstones	Grand Total
Aquarium Guides: Tropical Fish Species Guide			6.9	6.9
Computer Training: Office 365	19.92	59.76		79.68
Fundamentals of Mac OS Yosemite			6.82	6.82
Fundamentals of Mac OS: El Capitan			6.06	6.06
Fundamentals of Office 365	77.14	11.02	6.98	95.14
Fundamentals of Office 365: 2016 Edition	26.88		10.92	37.8
The Beginner's Guide to OFFICE 365			6.94	6.94
Tropical Fish: Setup & Maintenance Guide			6.02	6.02
Grand Total	123.94	70.78	50.64	245.36

How about the number of books sold? We can answer this question by adding the 'units sold' field.

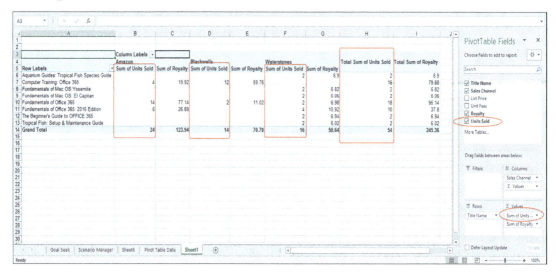

This might be a bit confusing to read. To make the data analysis easier, Excel has a feature called slicers.

Using Slicers

A slicer is essentially a filter, and allows you to filter the data in the pivot table to make things easier to analyse.

In the above example, we can see both units sold and the royalties for each sales channel, all on one table. To make things easier to analyse, we can add a slicer for sales channels that will enable us to select a sales channel, and display a pivot table for only that channel.

This helps break your data down into more concise parts.

To insert a slicer, click any cell in your pivot table, go to the 'pivot table analyse' ribbon tab and click 'insert slicer'.

From the 'insert slicers' panel that opens up, click the field you want to organise the data by. In this example we are organising the data by sales channel, so click 'sales channel'.

You'll see a slicer pop up with three sales channels, Amazon, Blackwells and Waterstones.

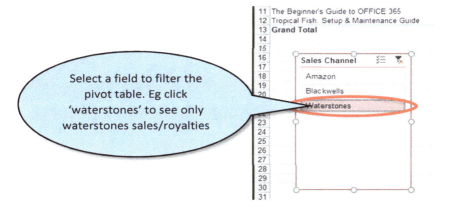

You can select multiple selections in the slicer by holding down the control key while you click.

Now, you'll see your slicer appear on your worksheet.

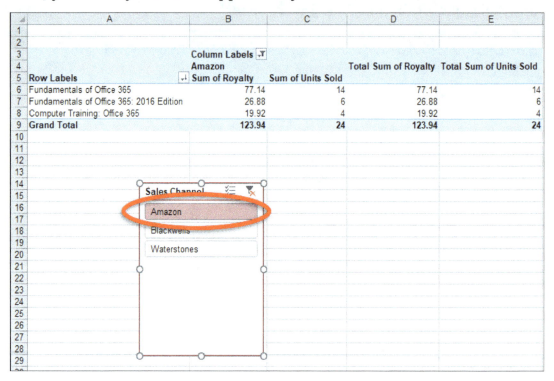

If you select 'amazon' you'll see all sales, etc from the amazon channel.

Similarly if you select 'blackwells' or 'waterstones' you'll see sales from those channels.

If you select all of the channels - remember hold down the control key on your keyboard to select multiple options - you'll see sales from all channels.

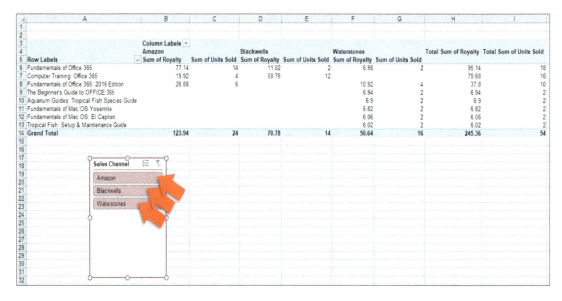

Sorting Pivot Table Data

You can also sort data in these tables in the same way you'd sort any column in your spreadsheet.

Say we wanted to find the best selling book?

I can adjust my pivot table to show total books sold (just need 'title name' and 'units sold' fields).

Now click in the 'sum of units sold' field, in the pivot table.

Row Labels	Sum of Units Sold
Aquarium Guides: Tropical Fish Species Guide	2
Computer Training: Office 365	
Fundamentals of Mac OS Yosemite	
Fundamentals of Mac OS: El Capitan	2
Fundamentals of Office 365	18
Fundamentals of Office 365: 2016 Edition	10
The Beginner's Guide to OFFICE 365	2
Tropical Fish: Setup & Maintenance Guide	2
Grand Total	54

Go to your data ribbon and click the 'descending' sort icon.

We can see the best seller is 'Fundamentals of Office 365'.

Row Labels	Sum of Units Sold
Fundamentals of Office 365	18
Computer Training: Office 365	16
Fundamentals of Office 365: 2016 Edition	10
Tropical Fish: Setup & Maintenance Guide	2
The Beginner's Guide to OFFICE 365	2
Fundamentals of Mac OS Yosemite	2
Aquarium Guides: Tropical Fish Species Guide	2
Fundamentals of Mac OS: El Capitan	2
Grand Total	54

Pivot Table Calculations

A useful feature of Pivot Tables is the ability to perform calculations without using any formulas.

Let's assume you have a dataset of sales data for different products over various months. Have a look at pivottablecalc.xlsx

First select the entire range of your data.

Click on the 'Insert' ribbon tab then select 'pivot chart'.

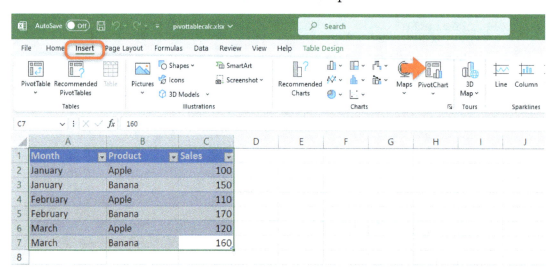

Delete the 'pivot chart' that appears. We don't need that at this stage.

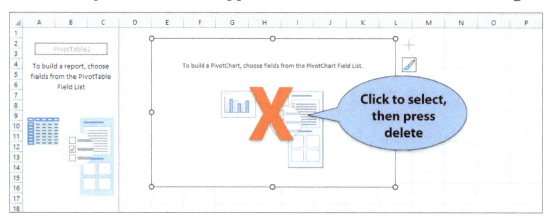

Using the panel on the right hand side we can construct the pivot table

1. Drag "Month" to Rows field area.
2. Drag "Product" to Columns field area.
3. Drag "Sales" to Values field area.

We end up with something like this:

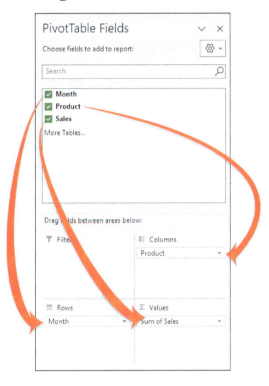

Now for the calculation. If you want the average sales, click on the drop-down arrow next to "Sum of Sales" in the sidebar on the right hand side. Choose 'Value Field Settings' from the drop down menu.

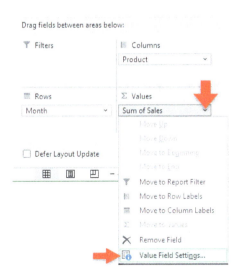

Select 'average'. Your PivotTable will now show average sales. If you want to see the count of entries instead, choose "Count". Try some of the other functions.

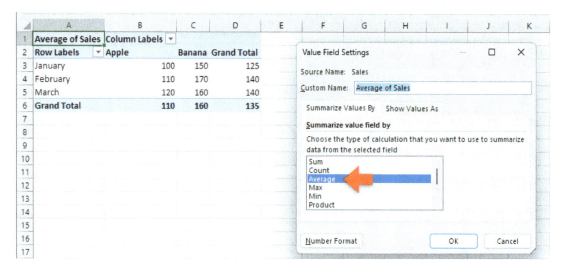

Filters

Filters provide a way to narrow down or focus on specific parts of your dataset without altering the source data. They are extremely useful for analyzing subsets of your data, comparing specific sections, or simply decluttering your PivotTable to present or view relevant insights.

Using the pivot table we created in the previous section, we can add a filter. Lets say we want to filter the sales data for a specific month. T apply it as a filter, drag 'Month' to the 'Filters' area.

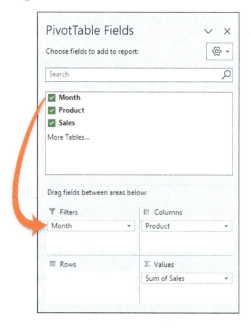

You'll see a drop down menu appear at the top of your pivot table. Click on the down arrow and select a month to apply the filter.

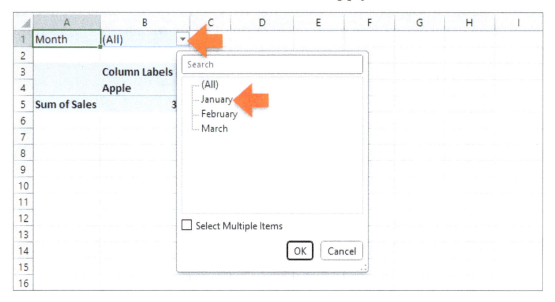

Suppose you only want to see sales for "Banana". Click on the dropdown arrow next to 'column labels'.

Uncheck 'all', then check "Apple". Click 'ok' when you're done.

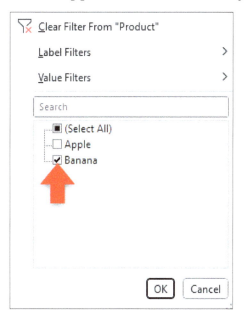

Pivot Charts

Pivot charts are pretty much the same thing as regular charts, covered earlier, except they represent data in a pivot table rather than a regular worksheet.

You add your charts in a similar fashion. First click on your pivot table and from the 'pivot table analyse' ribbon tab, select 'pivot chart'.

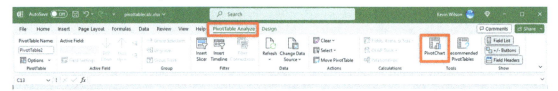

From the dialog box that appears, select a chart that is most appropriate for the data you are trying to illustrate. You can choose from pie charts, column or bar charts and line charts.

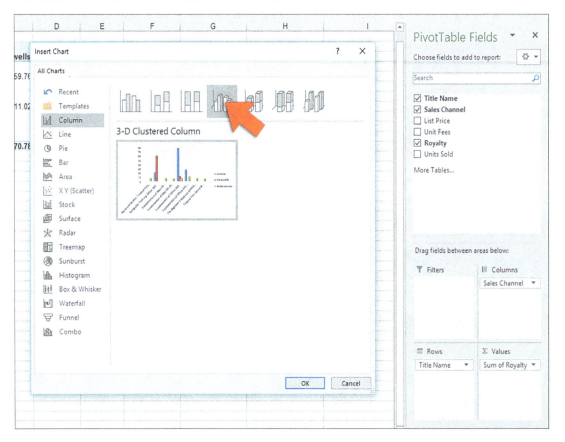

For this example, I'm going to add a nice 3D column chart.

As you can see from the chart, things can be a bit difficult to read on this particular chart. All three sales channels are on the same chart.

It would be nice if we can view them separately. Excel allows you to use slicers, which is essentially a filter.

In this example I am going to filter the chart by sales channel. So from the 'pivot table analyse' ribbon tab, click 'insert slicer'. From the dialog box that appears, select sales channel and click OK.

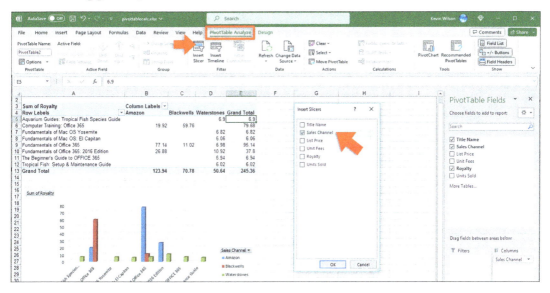

In the popup box that appears, I can select each of my sales channels in turn and take a closer look at the sales data.

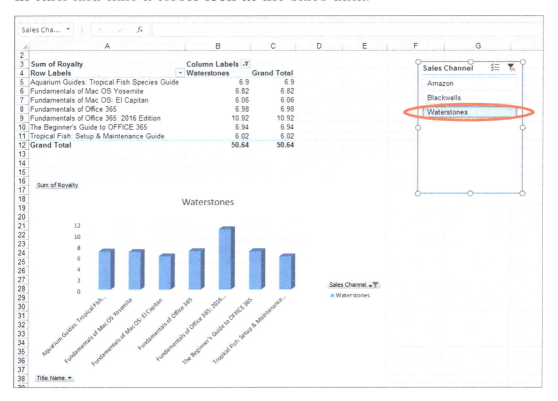

Try experimenting with adding different fields to different boxes on the 'PivotTable Fields' sidebar and see how it affects the pivot table.

You might have something like this...

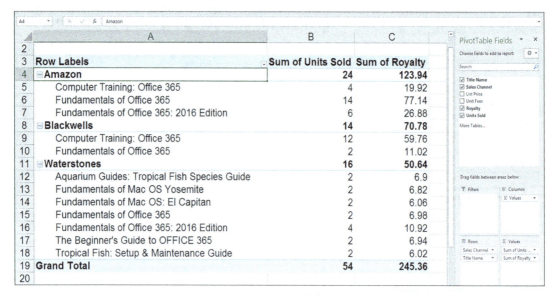

Notice where the fields are on the bottom half of the 'PivotTable Fields' sidebar in relation to the pivot chart.

Give it a try.

Analysis ToolPak

The Analysis ToolPak is an add-in for Microsoft Excel that allows you to perform various statistical, engineering, and financial analyses. Once enabled, you can execute complex data analysis procedures, such as regression, correlation, and hypothesis testing, without the need for specialized software.

To enable the add-in, go to 'file', select 'options'. Click on 'add-ins'. At the bottom, select 'excel add-ins', then click 'go'.

Check "Analysis ToolPak". Click 'ok'

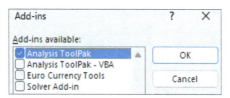

Imagine you have a list of sales figures for twelve months and you want to obtain a summary of the data, including the mean, median, mode, standard deviation, and range. Have a look at analysispak.xlsx

From the 'data' ribbon tab, go to the 'analysis group', then click on 'Data Analysis'. In the 'Data Analysis' dialog box, select 'Descriptive Statistics', then click 'ok'.

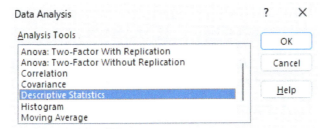

For the Input Range, select cells B1 through B12.

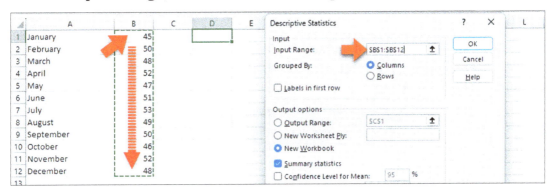

For the Output Range, enter D1. This is where the analysis statistics will appear. You can also select 'new worksheet' if you what the stats to appear on a separate worksheet.

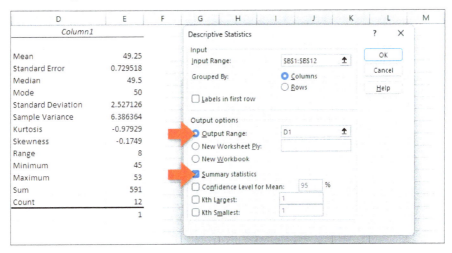

Check 'Summary statistics', then click 'ok'.

Solver

Solver is an add-in tool used for analytical purposes, particularly in addressing complex problems and assisting in decision-making within a business context. It operates by identifying the objective cell, decision variable cells, and constraints. By adjusting the values in the decision variable cells, Solver is able to find the optimal solution that meets the constraints and maximizes or minimizes the objective cell value, depending on the goal specified.

The Objective Cell is the cell containing the formula you wish to maximize, minimize, or achieve a certain value for.

Variable Cells are the cells that Solver will change to seek the optimal solution.

Constraints are the conditions or limitations under which the problem must be solved.

To use Solver, first you'll need to enable it. To enable the add in, go to 'file', select 'options'. Click on 'add-ins'. At the bottom, select 'excel add-ins', then click 'go'.

Check "Solver Add-in". Click 'ok'

Let's take a look at an example, suppose you run a small business who produces two types of products: Product X and Product Y.

Your goal is to maximize your profit.

The profit from each unit of Product X is £20 and from each unit of Product Y is £30.

However, you have constraints of a maximum of 200 labor hours available and each unit of Product X requires 2 labor hours while each unit of Product Y requires 3 labor hours to produce.

Have a look at solver.xlsx

Go to the 'data' ribbon tab, click on 'solver'. In the 'solver parameters' dialog box, set the objective. Click in the 'set objective' field, then click on cell C6 (where the Total Profit is calculated). In the 'to' field, select 'max' from the selections since you want to maximize profit.

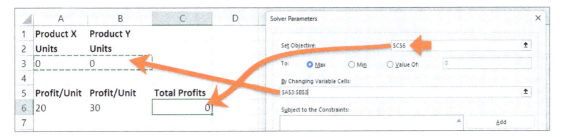

Click in the 'by changing variable cells field, then click and select cells A3 and B3 (these cells represent the number of units of Product X and Product Y respectively).

To add the constraint, 'add'. Click in the 'cell reference box', then click on cell C9 (This cell calculates the total labor hours). Select '<=' from the drop-down. In the constraint field type 200 (This is the maximum labor hours available).

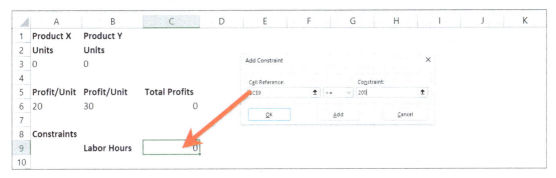

Click 'ok' on the 'add constraint' dialog box, then 'solve'.

Solver adjusts the quantities of Product X and Product Y to maximize profit while ensuring the total labor hours do not exceed 200. By changing the values in cells A3 and B3, Solver finds the optimal number of units to produce for each product. Once it finds the optimal solution, it displays these quantities in cells A3 and B3, and the maximum profit in cell C6.

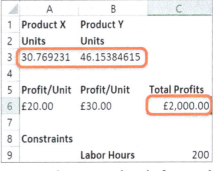

This provides a data-driven approach to make informed decisions on how to allocate resources effectively to achieve the highest profit.

7

Data Validation

Data Validation is a feature that allows you to set specific constraints on the data that can be entered into a cell or a range of cells. This ensures that the data collected or entered adheres to certain standards or conditions, enhancing data integrity and consistency.

In this chapter we'll take a look at

- Data Validation Rules
- By Data Type
- Text Length
- Custom Rules
- Displaying Messages
- Input & Error Message
- Create a Drop Down List
- Locking & Unlocking Cells

To help you better understand this section, take a look at the video resources. Open your web browser and navigate to the following website:

elluminetpress.com/exc-val

You'll also need to download the source files from:

elluminetpress.com/excel

Types of Validation

Data validation helps maintain data integrity by ensuring that the data entered conforms to certain criteria. Types of data validation include:

- **Whole Number** restricts the entry to whole numbers within a specified range.

- **Decimal** allows only decimal numbers within a specified range.

- **List** enables a dropdown list for the user to select a value from.

- **Date** restricts the entry to a date, with the ability to specify a range.

- **Time** allows only time values, with the ability to specify a range.

- **Text Length** ensures the text entered is within a specified length range.

- **Custom** allows for the creation of custom validation criteria using formulas.

Each type serves a unique purpose, making it easier to manage different kinds of data input, from restricting entries to numerical values within a specified range, to allowing selections from a predefined list.

For example, in the spreadsheet below, we could add a simple rule to the cell that contains number of items so it only allows whole numbers. This will prevent someone ordering 2 and a half items.

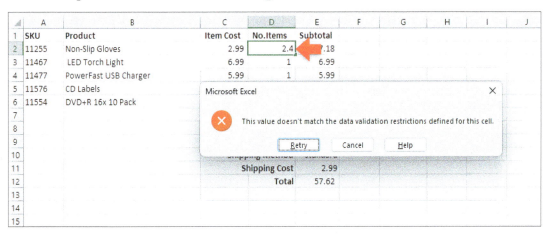

For advanced users, custom validation provides a powerful tool to create complex validation rules using formulas and even integrating VBA (Visual Basic for Applications) code.

Using these validation types, you can create validation rules to ensure accuracy and efficiency in data entry.

Validation Rules

In Excel, you can set a variety of rules to cells to help users enter the correct data. This feature allows you to set up rules and restrictions on the data that can be entered into specific cells. This helps to maintain data integrity and ensures that only valid and desired values are inputted.

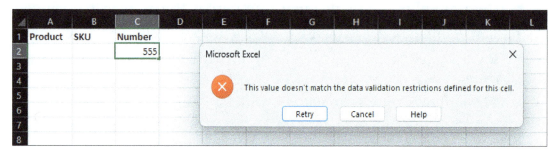

As you can see in the example above, a validation rule was added to C2 which only allows a whole number between 1 and 500. The user entered 555 which is larger than 500 so is out of range.

Lets take a look at an example in the **Data Validation Demo.xlsx** workbook.

By Data Type

Whole numbers are called integers in Excel and do not have any decimal places. In the example, we can add a validation check to the 'number of items' column. It's safe to assume that these will only be whole numbers, don't think anyone will try order half an LED torch light.

Select the cells you want to apply the validation check to. Go to your data ribbon and click 'data validation'

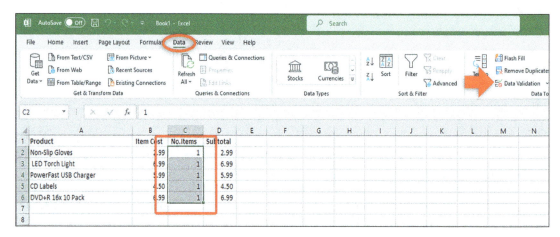

From the dialog box, click the drop down box under 'allow' and select 'whole number', because we only want to allow whole numbers in these cells.

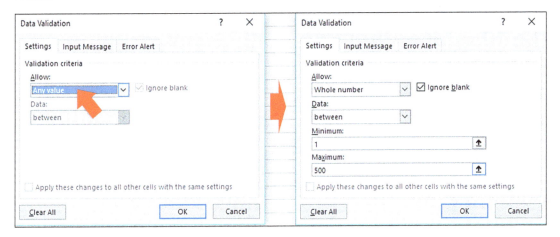

You can also set a criteria for the whole numbers. For example, we could set a range 1 - 500. We could argue that you can't order 0 items on the order form. We also set the maximum limit to 500 - meaning a customer can order up to 500 items at a time. So in the data field, select 'between'. Set the minimum value to 1 and the max value to 500.

If there was no maximum limit to the number of items ordered. Instead of selecting 'between' in the data field, you could select 'greater than or equal to' and set the minimum value to 1.

Text Length

You can enforce a specific length of text or numbers with data validation. In our example, we have a field called SKU, this is a unique product code each product in our catalogue has to identify it. In this case, each SKU is exactly 5 digits long and can't be more than 5 or less than 5 digits.

Select the cells you want to apply the validation to, in this example, it's the SKU column.

	A	B	C	D	E	F
1	SKU	Product	Item Cost	No.Items	Subtotal	
2	11255	...-Slip Gloves	2.99	4	11.96	
3	11467	...Torch Light	6.99	1	6.99	
4	11477	PowerFast USB Charger	5.99	1	5.99	
5	11576	CD Labels	4.50	3	13.50	
6	11554	DVD+R 16x 10 Pack	6.99	3	20.97	
7						
8						

Chapter 7: Data Validation

Go to your data ribbon and select 'data validation'.

From the dialog box, in the 'allow' field, select 'text length'.

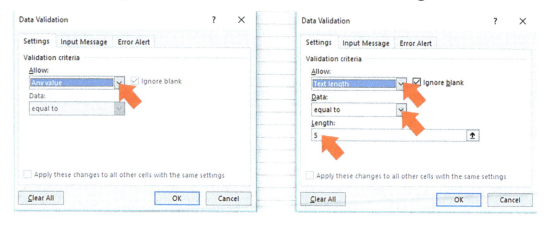

In the 'data' field, select 'equal to', because we want the text length equal to a certain length.

In the 'length' field, select 5. We want the length of the entries to be equal to 5 characters long.

Now when you try type in a number that has more or less than 5 characters, you will get an error message.

Create a Drop Down List

Drop down lists allow the user to select pre-set options allocated to a particular cell, instead of having to type the data in.

If we take a look at an example in the **Data Validation Demo.xlsx** workbook

To create a drop down list, select the cell you want the drop down list to appear in.

6	DVD+R 16x 10 Pack		6.99	3	20.97
7					
8					
9				Net Total	59.41
10				Shipping Method	Standard
11				Shipping Cost	2.99
12				Total	62.40

From the Data tab, click the Data Validation.

From the dialog box that appears, in the allow field, click in the drop down, and from the options select 'list'.

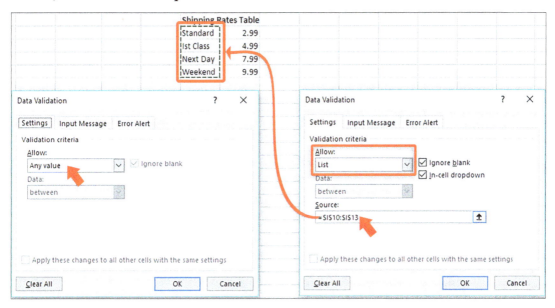

Click in the 'source' field that appears, and select the range of values that you want the user to be able to choose from, in the drop down box we're creating. Click OK when you're done

You'll notice a little down arrow appear next to the cell we selected. Click the arrow to select the desired option and see what happens.

Custom

Custom validation allows you to create your own validation rules based on formulas. This is particularly useful when the built-in validation options do not meet your needs. Let's assume you are managing a small project and need to ensure that the end date of a task is after its start date.

To set up custom validation, select the cells under the "End Date" column.

On 'data' ribbon tab, click 'data validation'.

Chapter 7: Data Validation

In the 'data validation' dialog box, under the 'settings tab, select 'custom' from the 'allow' dropdown menu.

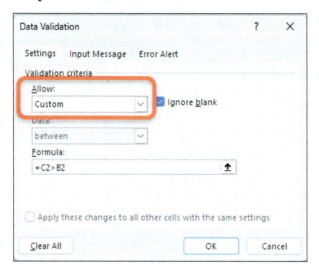

In the 'formula' box, type in an equals sign (=), then select the cell with the end date for Task 1 (C2). Enter a greater than sign, then click the cell with the start date (B2). You'll end up with the formula: =C2>B2. This ensures that the end date (C2) of a task is after the start date (B2). Click 'ok' to apply the validation.

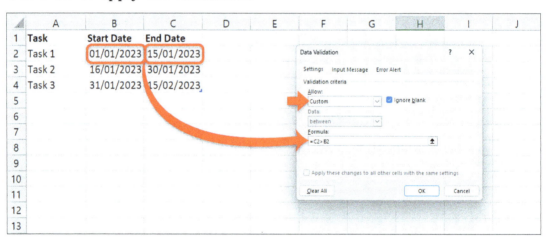

Now, when you try and enter an end date that comes before the start date, you get an error

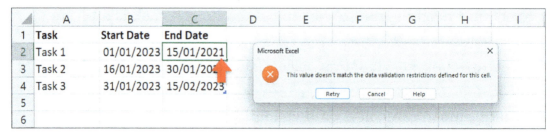

Displaying Messages

You can display messages to your users if they input invalid data and messages explaining what data is required.

If we take a look at an example in the **Data Validation Demo.xlsx** workbook

Input Message

Input messages appear, telling the user what data is expected, when the cell is selected. Going back to our example, remember we added a validation check to the 'number of items' column to accept whole numbers between 1 and 500. We can add an input message to explain this to the user.

To do this, select the cells in the 'number of items' column.

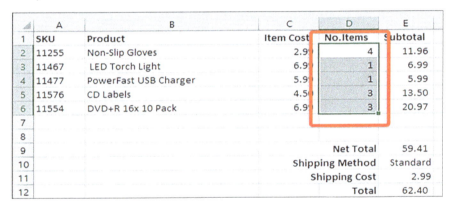

From the data ribbon click 'data validation'.

From the dialog box go to the 'input message' tab.

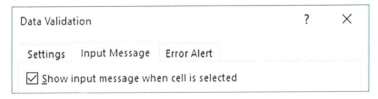

Check the check box next to 'Show input message when cell is selected', so the message appears when the user clicks on one of the cells.

In the title field enter a title. This could be the name of the column.

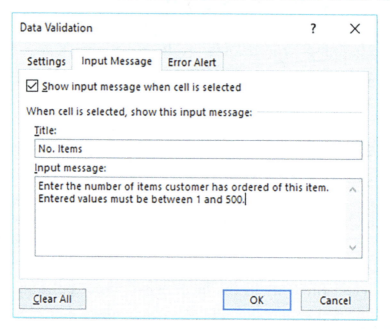

In the 'input message' field, enter the message. This is a brief description of the field and the data that is required from the user. Click OK when you're done.

When the user clicks on a cell, they'll see the message pop up.

SKU	Product	Item Cost	No.Items	Subtotal
11255	Non-Slip Gloves	2.99	4	11.96
11467	LED Torch Light	6.99		
11477	PowerFast USB Charger	5.99		
11576	CD Labels	4.50		
11554	DVD+R 16x 10 Pack	6.99		
		Net Total		59.41
		Shipping Method		Standard
		Shipping Cost		2.99
		Total		62.40

No. Items
Enter the number of items customer has ordered of this item. Entered values must be between 1 and 500.

Error Messages

If the user enters invalid data, you can alert then using an error message.

If we take a look at an example in the **Data Validation Demo.xlsx** workbook

To do this, select the cells in the 'number of items' column.

	A	B	C	D	E
1	SKU	Product	Item Cost	No Items	Subtotal
2	11255	Non-Slip Gloves	2.99	4	11.96
3	11467	LED Torch Light	6.99	1	6.99
4	11477	PowerFast USB Charger	5.99	1	5.99
5	11576	CD Labels	4.50	3	13.50
6	11554	DVD+R 16x 10 Pack	6.99	3	20.97
7					
8					
9				Net Total	59.41
10				Shipping Method	Standard
11				Shipping Cost	2.99
12				Total	62.40

From the data ribbon click 'data validation'.

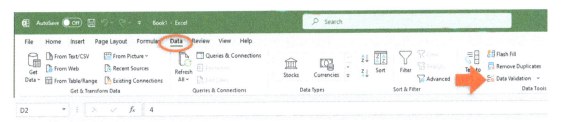

From the dialog box that appears click the 'error alert' tab.

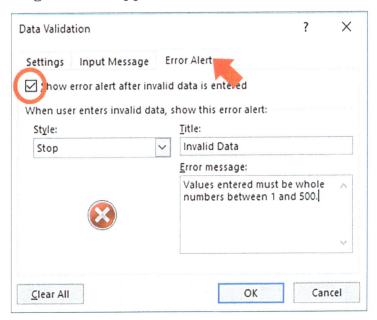

Click the check box next to 'Show error alert after invalid data is entered', so the message appears when the user clicks on one of the cells.

Chapter 7: Data Validation

In the title field enter a title. This could be the name of the column.

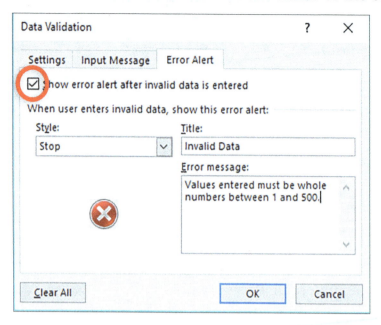

In the 'error message' field, enter the message. This is the message you want to display to the user, type a reminder in here as to what data is expected for that cell.

In the style field. Select the type of error message you want to show. An error, warning or an info box. You have Stop, Warning and Info as shown below.

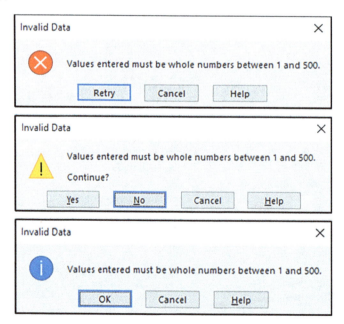

Click OK when you're done. If the user enters invalid data, they'll see the dialog box pop up.

Locking Cells

When your users are using your spreadsheet, they may accidentally wipe out formulas and cells you don't really want them to change.

Excel allows you to lock cells and cell ranges so your users can't change the contents. If we take a look at an example in the **Data Validation Demo.xlsx** workbook, it would make the spreadsheet more resilient to errors if we locked all the cells with formulas, shipping data, and totals, so the user can't change them.

To do this, select the cells the user is allowed to enter data. In the example, this would be: SKU, Product, Item Cost, and No. Items. To include the shipping option, hold down the control key then click on the shipping method.

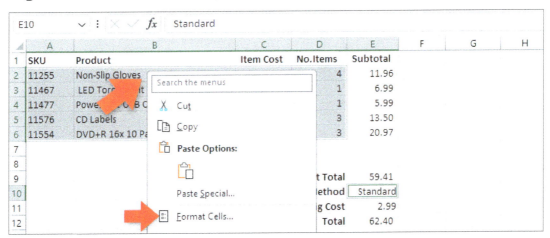

Right click on the selection, then select 'format cells' from the menu.

Go to the 'protection' tab. Click the check box next to 'locked' to remove it. This will unlock the selected cells. Click 'ok' when you're done.

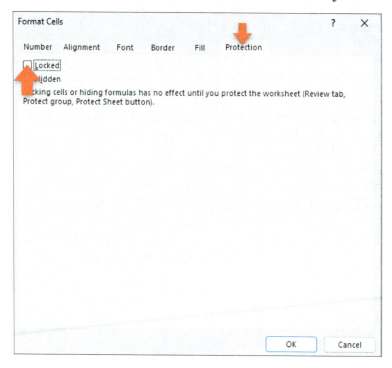

Now we need to protect the worksheet. To do this, go to the 'review' ribbon tab. Click 'protect sheet'.

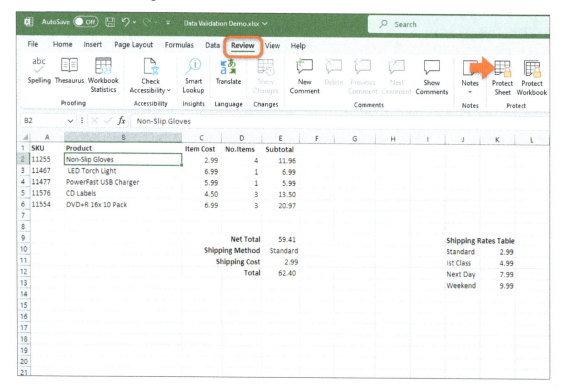

In the 'protect sheet' dialog box, at the top, enter a password to unprotect the sheet. This means that you'll need to enter this password if you want to unprotect the sheet to make changes to protected cells.

Make sure the box next to 'protect worksheet and contents of locked cells' is checked. Click 'ok' when you're done.

If you set a password, you'll need to re-enter it in the next dialog box for confirmation.

Unlocking Cells

To unlock cells, go to the 'review' ribbon tab. Click 'unprotect sheet'.

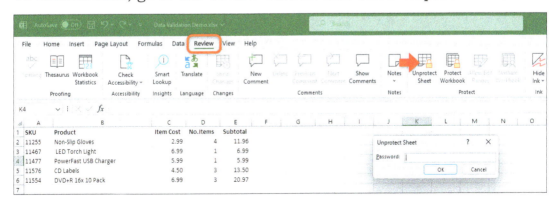

If a password was set, you will need to enter it.

Sharing & Collabora-tion

Sharing involves actively providing other users access to a document, enabling them to view or edit, based on defined permissions.

Collaboration is a collective, interactive effort where multiple individuals work together on a shared workbook by contributing ideas, feedback, and making edits in real-time.

To share and collaborate, you'll need a Microsoft account. Anyone you share the workbook with will also need a Microsoft account. Also, workbooks need to be saved on OneDrive or SharePoint to enable real-time collaboration.

The person sharing the workbook can set specific permissions, determining whether recipients can edit, comment on, or only view the document.

You'll need to download the source files from:

elluminetpress.com/excel

Introduction

Microsoft Office applications such as Word, Excel, and PowerPoint allow You to save your files directly to OneDrive, making it easy to access files across all your devices.

On your PC/Mac, OneDrive creates a special folder that is synchronized with your OneDrive cloud storage. Any files or folders that you save to the OneDrive folder on your PC will automatically be uploaded to the cloud, and any changes made to files in the cloud will be copied back to the OneDrive folder on your PC. This is called synchronisation.

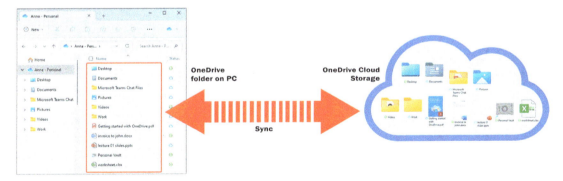

On mobile devices you can access all your OneDrive files without having to download them all to your device. This is called 'Files On-Demand'. This means all of your files and folders on OneDrive will be visible, but they are not be downloaded to your device until you actually need them. This feature saves space on your device and allows you to access your files from anywhere, even if you don't have enough storage on your local device.

OneDrive comes pre-installed on Windows 10/11 and you can access it through the File Explorer.

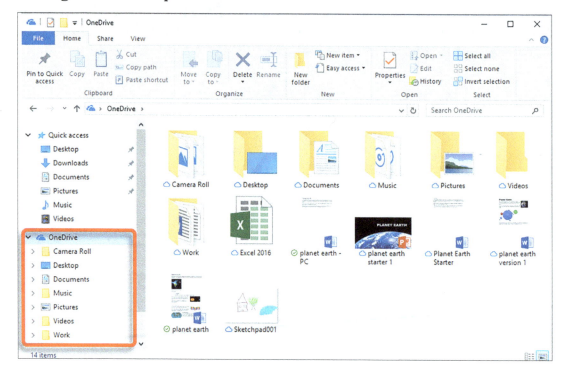

On a Mac, you can download the OneDrive app from the App Store. You'll find a OneDrive folder in the Finder app, and a shortcut to the OneDrive app along the top of the menu bar.

You can install the OneDrive app on mobile devices such as iPhones, iPads, and Android devices using the App Store.

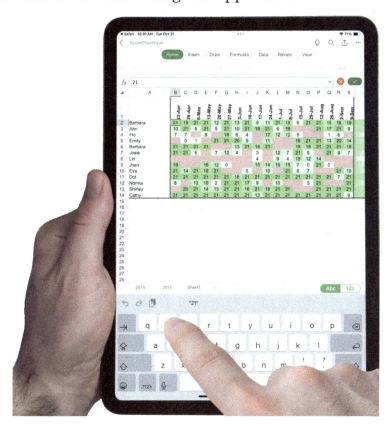

You can access OneDrive on the web using a web browser such as Chrome, Safari or Edge.

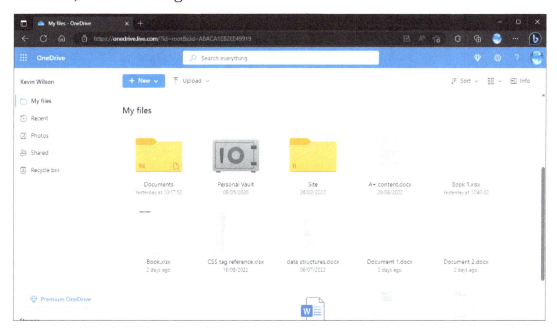

Collaborating in Excel

Collaborating in Microsoft Excel is a straightforward process. You can collaborate with others through the usual office apps such as Word, Excel and PowerPoint as well as Microsoft Teams, SharePoint, and OneDrive. For example, you can share an Excel workbook with someone else using OneDrive.

Sharing a Workbook

To do this, click 'share' on the top right of your screen. You can do this in Word, Excel and PowerPoint. From the drop down menu select 'share'.

In this example, I'm going to share the workbook with someone else. To do this, type in the person's email address, then type in a message below if applicable.

On the right hand side of the window, you'll see some sharing options. Select whether people will be able to edit the document or just view. In this example, I'm going to allow edits. Click send.

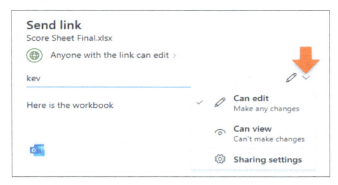

When your friend/colleague checks their email, they will be invited to open the workbook. Click 'open' or 'view in OneDrive' to open.

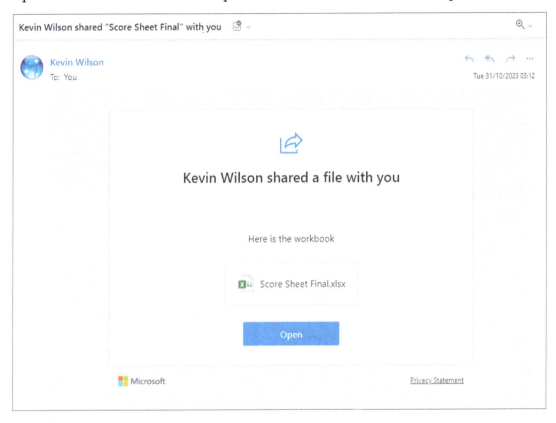

They will also see the workbook listed in the 'shared with me' section on the home screen when you start the Excel desktop app.

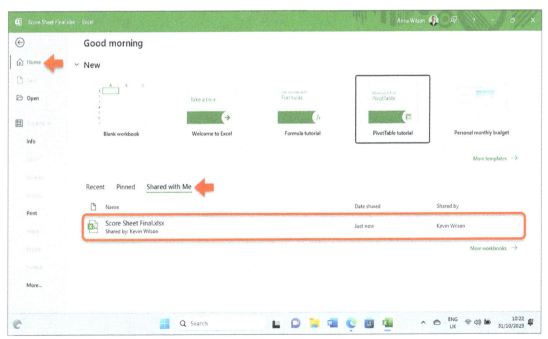

From here, your colleague/friend can edit or view the workbook. If they have Excel installed on their machine, they can download and work on the workbook in Excel. If they don't, they can work on the workbook online, within their web browser.

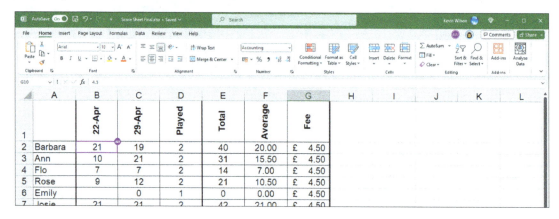

This is useful if you are working on a project with more than one person. Each person you shared the workbook with can edit and add content.

Real-Time Co-Authoring

Once you've opened a shared workbook, you'll see the other person's avatar appear in the menu bar on the top right of the screen. Here, you can jump to the location in the worksheet this person is working on, or you can send them an email message.

You can see the other person's edits or where they are in the worksheet as indicated by these markers with their name on it.

	A	B 22-Apr	C 29-Apr	D Played	E Total	F Average	G Fee	
2	Barbara	21	19	2	40	20.00	£	4.50
3	Ann	10	21	2	31	15.50	£	4.50
4	Flo	7	7	2	14	7.00	£	4.50
5	Rose	9	12	2	21	10.50	£	4.50
6	Emily		0	1	0	0.00	£	4.50
7	Josie	21	21	2	42	21.00	£	4.50
8	Lin			0	0	0.00	£	4.50
9	Joan	19		1	19	19.00	£	4.50
10	Eva	21	14	2	35	17.50	£	4.50
11								

Commenting

You can add comments to parts of the workbook. To do this, first select & highlight the cells you want to comment on. Click 'comments' on the top right of the screen, then 'new'. In the comment dialog box, type in your comment, then click the post icon.

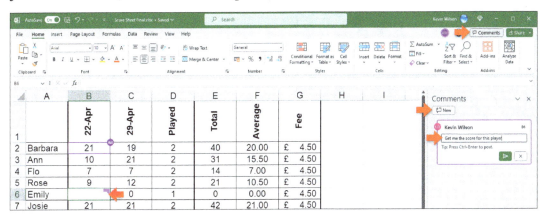

Your comment will appear in the comments sidebar linked to the highlighted text that was commented on.

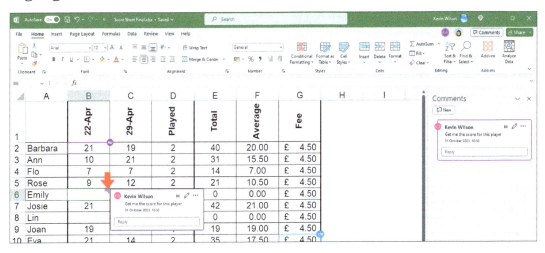

If you want to reply to the comment, type a message into the 'reply' field under the comment.

9

Managing Workbooks

Managing workbooks in Excel involves various tasks and skills that are crucial for effective spreadsheet organization and data management such as creating new workbooks, opening existing ones, saving, closing, printing and organizing them efficiently.

- Printing and Page Setup
- Margins
- Customising Margins
- Headers & Footers
- Page Print Order
- Print Options
- Print Row & Column Headers
- Print Gridlines
- Print Selection
- Print Titles
- Show & Print Formulas
- Opening a Saved Workbook
- Saving Workbooks
- Save as a Different Format
- Add-Ins

You'll need to download the source files from:

elluminetpress.com/excel

Printing your Spreadsheet

To print your document, click 'file' on the top left hand corner of the screen

From the menu on the left hand side of the screen, select print.

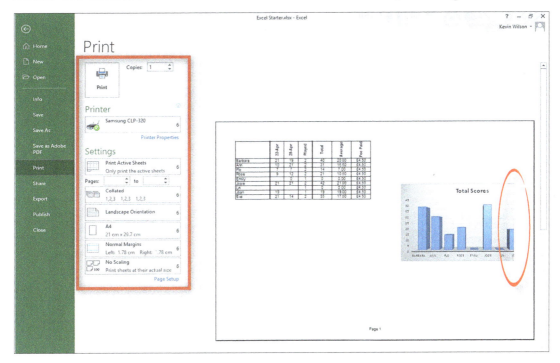

From the settings shown above, you can select the number of copies, the printer you're using, the range of pages you want to print. For example, if you just want to print the first page, last page etc.

You can select landscape or portrait paper orientation - use landscape for printing most spreadsheets.

Select paper size such as letter, legal, A3 or A4.

Margins, you can adjust from here. Select normal, wide margins or narrow margins.

Scaling can be used to make the spreadsheet bigger or smaller to fit your page.

When printing in Excel, keep an eye on the preview on the right hand side of the screen above. Notice how the chart is cut off. Sometimes columns can be cut off too. You can adjust this by going back to your spreadsheet- clicking the back arrow on the very top left of the screen. This will take you back to your spreadsheet.

Chapter 9: Managing Workbooks

Excel will have placed dotted lines showing the edge of the page print area. Move the content you want on the page inside this area, either by moving charts by dragging or resizing columns etc.

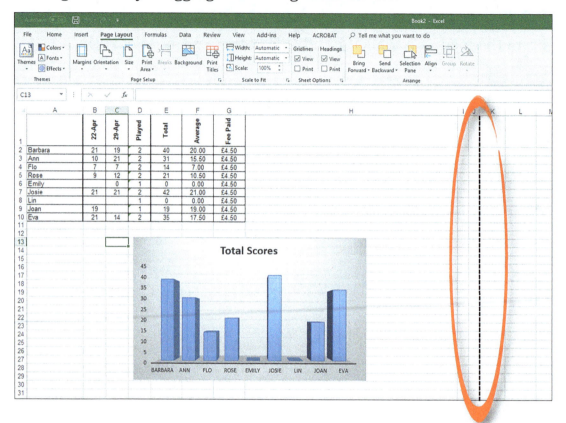

Also check your margins on the page layout ribbon, select narrow.

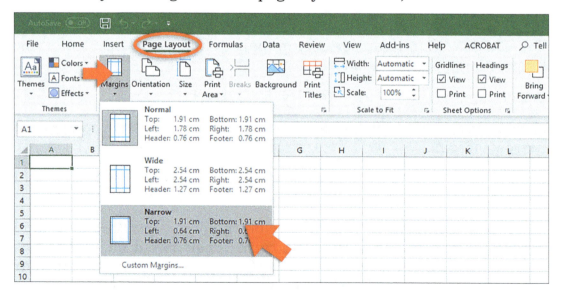

Now go to print your spreadsheet as before. (File -> Print).

Once you are happy with the print preview, print your document.

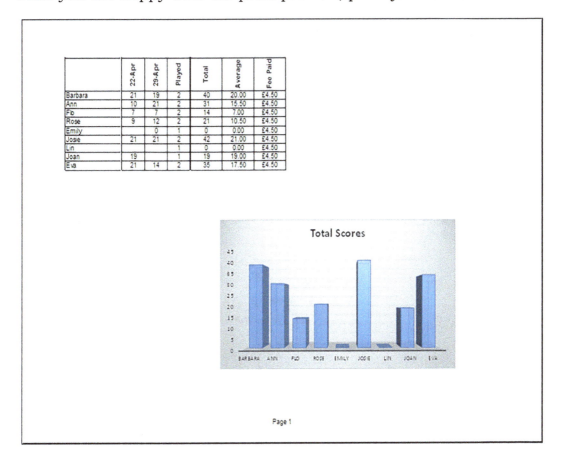

Click the print icon to send the spreadsheet to the printer.

You can make more detailed changes using the 'page setup' settings, in the following sections.

Page Setup

Page Setup allows you to customize the way your worksheet looks when it's printed. You can adjust settings such as page orientation, paper size, margins, headers, and footers.

To open the page setup options, click file. Then from the backstage that appears, click 'print'.

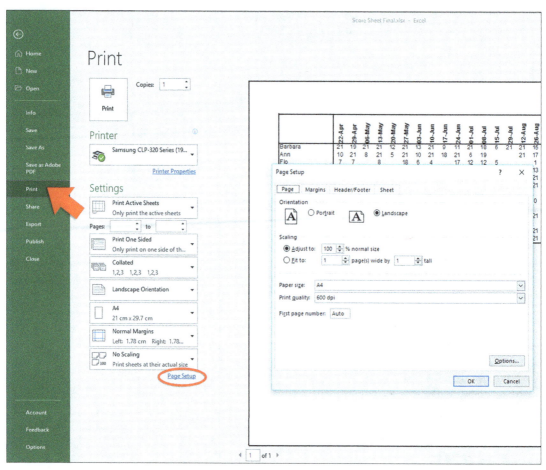

You'll see some basic settings listed down the left of the print window. These are usually the most used settings for changing number of copies printed, single sided or double sided print, orientation - landscape or portrait, paper size - legal or A4, margins and scaling - useful if your spreadsheet just doesn't fit on a page.

To open the full page setup options, click 'page setup' at the bottom of the screen, circled above.

You'll see a dialog box appear with four tabs across the top: page, margins, header/footer and sheet.

Page Options

From the page tab you can set page orientation to portrait or landscape.

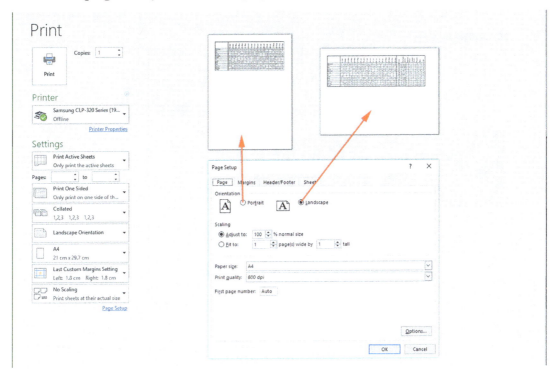

Underneath, you have some options for scaling your spreadsheet. This is useful if you want to shrink your spreadsheet down to fit onto one page. Do this by adjusting the size percentage in the 'adjust to...' field.

If you have quite a large spreadsheet that wont fit on one page, you can scale the spreadsheet across multiple pages. If we look at our example **Score Sheet Final.xlsx** on '2014' worksheet, you'll see that the sheet and the charts appear across 5 pages.

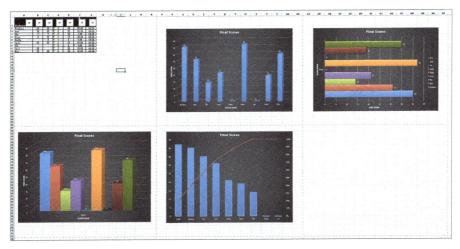

Chapter 9: Managing Workbooks

In the scaling section of the page tab, click fit to, then make sure it's set to **1** page wide by **1** page tall.

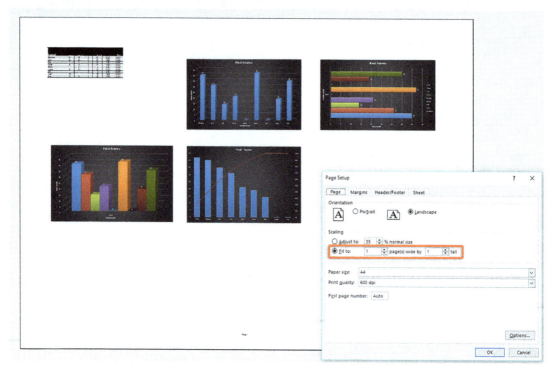

This will fit the spreadsheet to one page.

You can also use the shortcuts on the print screen settings section, as indicated below.

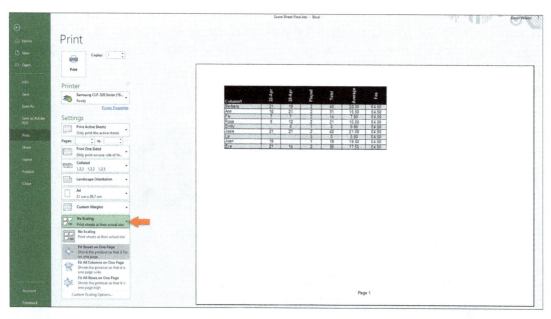

Click 'fit sheet on one page'.

Margins

The margin is the space between the data and the edge of the printed page.

In the illustration below, the top margins are shown in red, the left and right margins are shown in blue and the header/footer margins are shown in green.

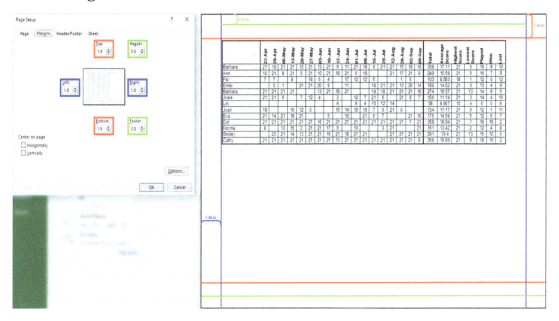

To adjust your margins, go to your page layout ribbon and click 'margins'. From the drop down menu, you can select some presets.

Wide margins give your more space around the edges of your document but you can fit less data on your page.

Narrow margins reduce the space around the edges and allows you to squeeze more onto your page - useful if your spreadsheet just doesn't fit on your page.

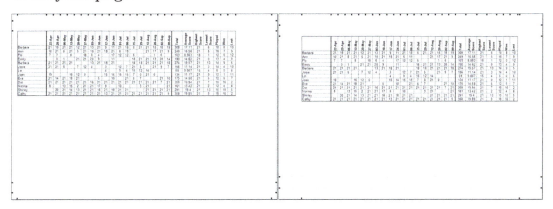

Customising Margins

You can customise your margins to your own specifications. A quick way to do this is to click file, then from the backstage click 'print'.

From the print preview screen, click the 'show margins' icon located on the bottom right of your screen.

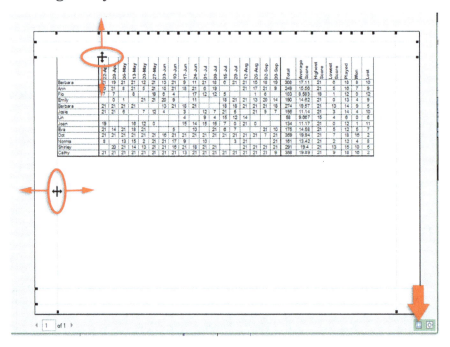

You'll see the margin lines appear on the preview. Click and drag the lines to adjust the margins.

Headers & Footers

Headers and footers appear at the top and bottom of your spreadsheet when it is printed out. You won't see any headers and footers when building your spreadsheet, unless you are in page layout mode.

To quickly edit your headers & footers, click on the 'page layout' icon on the bottom right of your screen. You'll see your spreadsheet on screen divide up into printable pages.

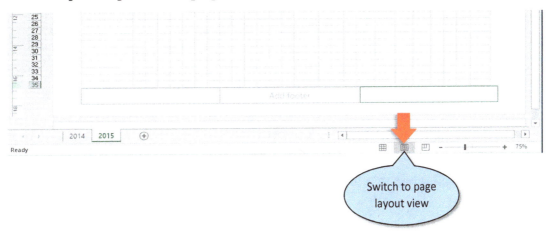

Along the top and bottom, you'll see place holders for your headers & footers. There are three boxes. Click in each of these to add headings.

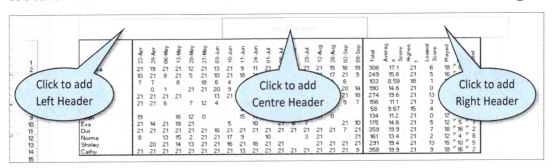

The left box is to add text to the left hand side, the centre box for centred text and the right hand box for right aligned text.

To add a header, click in one of these boxes. In this example, I am using the file **score sheet final.xlsx**. I am going to add the date to the left box, the title in the centre box and my initials to the right hand box.

Click in the left hand header box. When you click in one of these boxes, you'll notice a new ribbon appears called 'design'. This ribbon contains all your header and footer tools.

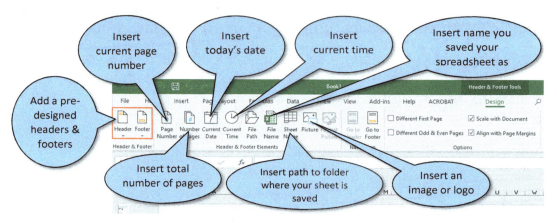

From the design ribbon click 'current date'. This will add today's date to the header box.

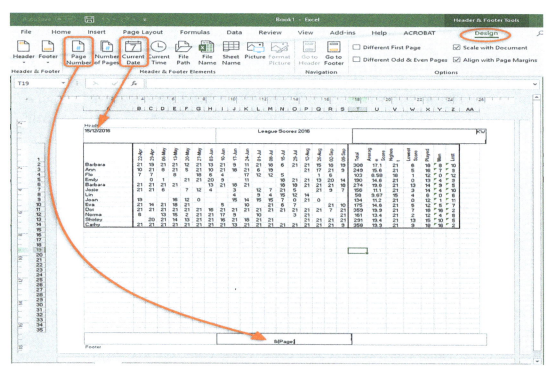

Click the centre box and type 'League Scores 2019' and in the right hand box type your initials. If you want to change the font or text size, you can do this from your home ribbon as normal.

To go to the footer, click in the footer section at the bottom of the page preview. Click the centre box, then from the design ribbon click 'page number.

Page Print Order

Click file, then select print from the backstage. Click 'page setup'. Select the 'sheet' tab.

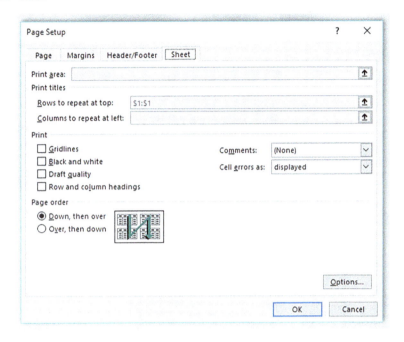

If we take a look at the page order section, this tells Excel in what order to print your spreadsheet if it's larger than one printed page. To explain what this means, if we come out of print preview and take a look at our spreadsheet, you'll notice that Excel has put in some dotted lines.

These lines are where Excel has divided your spreadsheet into pages according to your page size and orientation.

Lets have a look at an example with some data. Open **Score Sheet Final.xlsx** and open the '2014' worksheet.

If you select 'down then over' from the sheet tab on the page setup dialog box, your spreadsheet will print out in this order

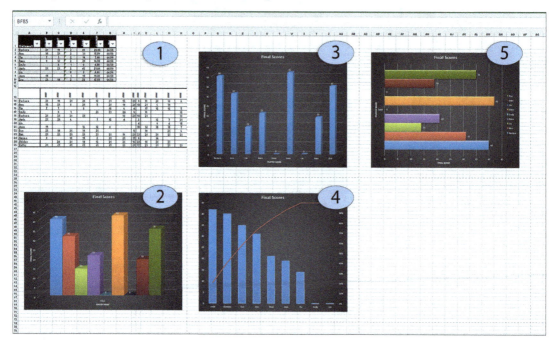

If you select 'over then down', your spreadsheet will print out like this

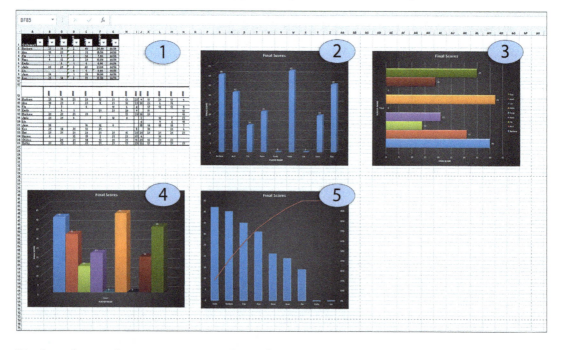

Notice the order pages are printed out.

Print Options

Excel provides various print options to help you customize the way your spreadsheets are printed. To view or change these options, click 'file' on the far left hand side, then select print from the panel on the left hand side.

Click 'page setup'. Select the 'sheet' tab.

Print Row and Column Headers

This prints the row and column reference headers, circled below. Excel doesn't print these by default but should you need to include them in a printout, you can turn them on from the sheet tab.

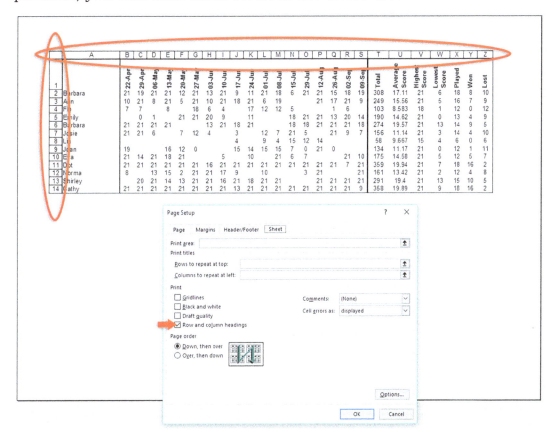

From the sheet tab in the page setup dialog box, go down to the print section and select 'row and column headings'.

Click OK when you're done.

Notice the column and row reference headers are visible in the print preview, shown above.

Print Gridlines

This feature prints the gridlines on your spreadsheets regardless if you have added borders when formatting your sheet.

Excel doesn't print these by default but should you need to include them in a printout, you can turn them on from the sheet tab. This feature can be useful for making data clearer in a printout.

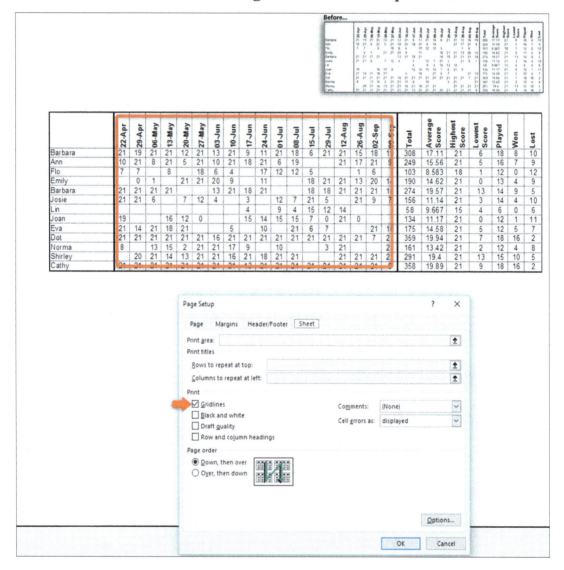

From the sheet tab in the page setup dialog box, go down to the print section and select 'gridlines'.

Click OK when you're done. Notice the gridlines are visible in the print preview as well as the border's we added when formatting our spreadsheet, as shown above.

Print Selection

Print selection allows you to select a specific part of your spreadsheet to print out. You do this by setting a print area.

To set a print area, highlight the area you want to print. In the example **Score Sheet Final.xlsx**, I want to print out the scores and the total, which is the first half of the score table. So highlight A1 to T14, as shown below.

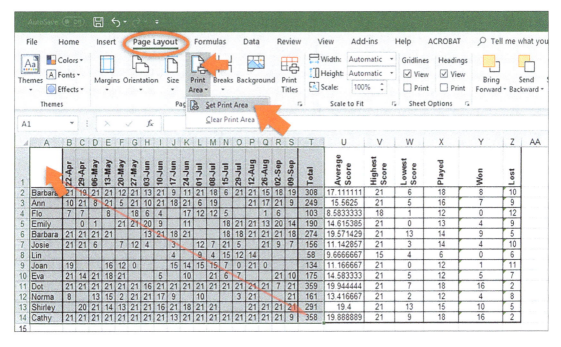

Go to your page layout ribbon and select 'print area'. From the drop down menu, click 'set print area'.

This will tell Excel that you only want to include this area in your printout.

	22-Apr	29-Apr	06-May	13-May	20-May	27-May	03-Jun	10-Jun	17-Jun	24-Jun	01-Jul	08-Jul	15-Jul	29-Jul	12-Aug	26-Aug	02-Sep	09-Sep	Total
Barbara	21	19	21	21	12	21	13	21	9	11	21	18	6	21	21	15	18	19	308
Ann	10	21	8	21	5	21	10	21	18	21	6	19			21	17	21	9	249
Flo	7	7		8		18	6	4		17	12	12	5			1	6		103
Emily		0	1		21	21	20	9		11			18	21	21	13	20	14	190
Barbara	21	21	21	21			13	21	18	21			18	18	21	21	21	18	274
Josie	21	21	6		7	12	4		3		12	7	21	5		21	9	7	156
Lin					4			15	14	15	15	7	0	21	0				58
Joan	19			16	12	0		15	14	15	15	7	0	21	0				134
Eva	21	14	21	18	21			5		10		21	6	7		21	10		175
Dot	21	21	21	21	21	21	16	21	21	21	21	21	21	21	21	7	21		359
Norma	8		13	15	2	21	21	17	9		10			3	21			21	161
Shirley		20	21	14	13	21	21	16	21	18	21	21			21	21	21	21	291
Cathy	21	21	21	21	21	21	21	21	13	21	21	21	21	21	21	21	21	9	358

Print Titles

If we take a look at our example bank statement **Statement Example. xlsx,** you'll notice when you go to print preview, it prints out over two pages. If you look at the second page, you'll see Excel has not printed the headings.

You can mark rows and columns you want to appear on each page using the print titles feature. To do this, go to your page layout ribbon and click 'print titles'.

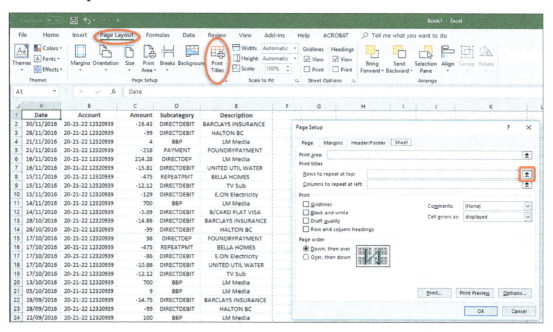

From the dialog box click the small arrow next to 'rows to repeat at top'. We want to repeat the top row on all pages - the column titles.

Now select the top row of the spreadsheet, then click the X on the top right of the small dialog box.

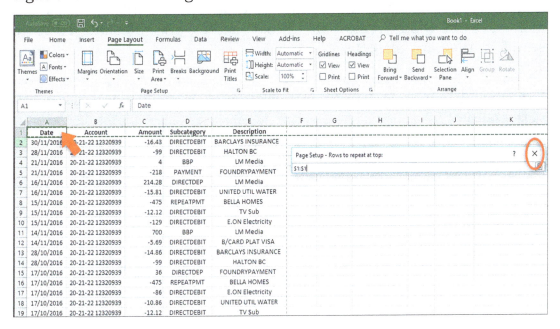

Click OK on dialog box that appears.

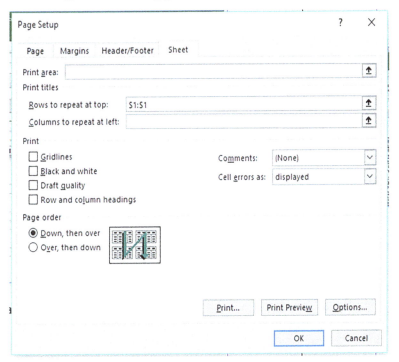

Now, when you go to print preview, you'll see that the top row appears on every page. You can do this with columns too, just select 'columns to repeat at left' from the dialog box instead of 'rows to repeat at top'.

Show & Print Formulas

Sometimes it's useful to be able to view the formulas themselves instead of the result. This helps proof reading and checking to make sure formulas are correct.

To show the formulas, go to your formulas ribbon and click 'show formulas'. To see the whole formula, you might have to adjust the width of the columns.

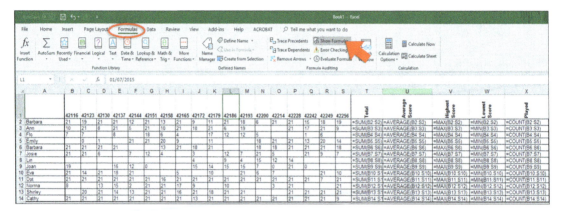

You can also print these formulas if you need to in the normal way. Click file then print.

When you print these formulas, you might need to do some scaling to make them fit onto one page. Use the scaling options at the bottom of the print preview window.

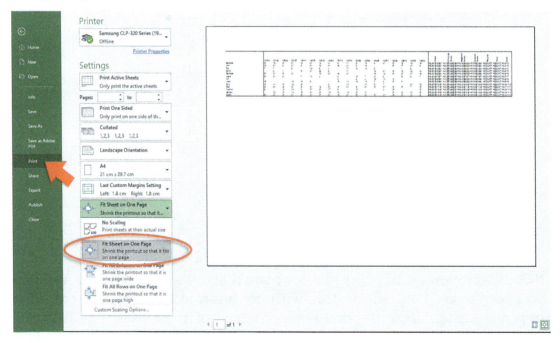

Opening a Saved Workbook

If Excel is already open you can open previously saved workbooks by clicking the FILE menu on the top left of your screen.

From the green bar along the left hand side click 'open', click 'OneDrive - Personal'.

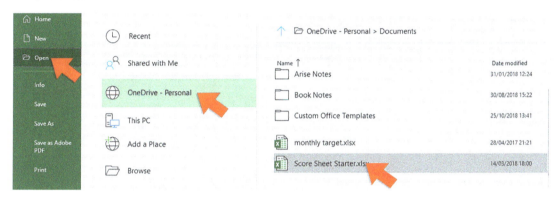

From the list, select the workbook you want to open. The workbook from a previous project was saved as 'excel final.xlsx', so this is the one I am going to open here. Double click the file name to open it.

For convenience, instead of searching through your OneDrive, Excel lists all your most recently opened Excel files. You can view these by selecting 'recent'. Selecting 'workbooks' shows your recently opened spreadsheets, 'folders' shows the folders of the spreadsheets recently opened

Your latest files will be listed first.

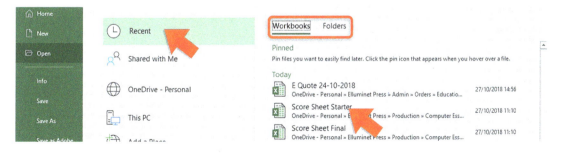

Double click the file name to open it.

Saving Workbooks

To save files, click the small disk icon in the top left hand corner of your screen.

Excel also has an auto save option. This means Excel will automatically save your workbook each time you make a change. To turn this feature on or off, click the 'autosave' icon.

Select your OneDrive - Personal, then select a folder you want to save the file into, eg 'documents'.

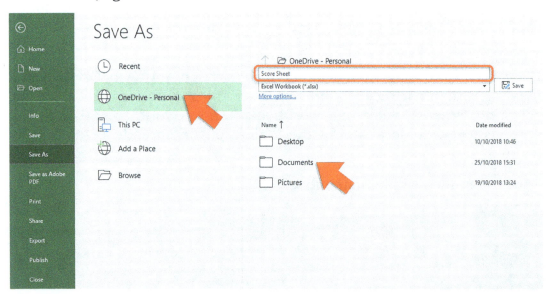

Enter a meaningful name in the text field indicated above by the red arrow.

Click save.

Save as a Different Format

You can save your Excel spreadsheets in different formats depending on what you want to do with the file. You can save as CSV, web pages, and PDFs.

To save files in a different format, eg PDF, click 'file'.

From the backstage, click 'save' or 'save a copy'. Then select OneDrive.

Select where you want to save the file.

Give the file a meaningful name.

Underneath, select the small down arrow next to the file type field. From the drop down menu, select the file format you want to use.

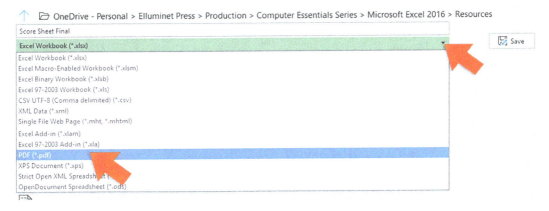

Click 'save' when you're done.

Add-Ins

Excel add-ins are third-party software components or extensions that add extra features and functionalities to Microsoft Excel. There are different types of Excel Add-Ins. Let's take a look at some examples

Com Add-Ins are built using COM (Component Object Model) that typically offer more advanced and integrated features. They can interact more deeply with Excel and are often created using programming languages like VBA (Visual Basic for Applications) or .NET.

Excel Add-Ins (XLL) add-ins are dynamic-link libraries (.xll) that provide custom functions or automation tools within Excel. They are particularly useful for creating complex calculations or data analysis tools.

Excel Add-Ins (VSTO) add-ins are designed using Visual Studio and are ideal for creating custom task panes, ribbon tabs, or other user interface elements.

Web Add-Ins are web-based and can be used in Excel Online and Excel for Office 365. They often use web technologies like HTML, JavaScript, and CSS.

Excel Add-Ins from the Office Store are easy to install and can extend Excel's functionality without requiring programming knowledge.

Installing

To install an Add-in, from on the 'home' ribbon tab select 'Add-ins'. From the drop down menu select 'get add-ins'.

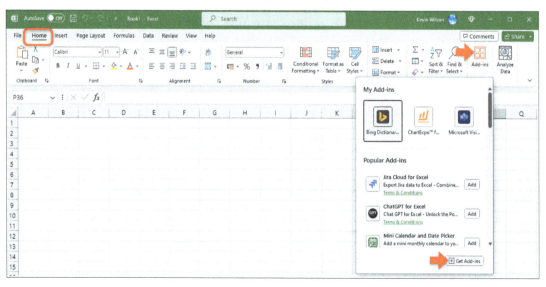

An 'office add-ins' window will open. Use the categories down the left hand side to browse, or you can also search using the 'search' field.

Once you have found the add-in you want to install, click on 'add'.

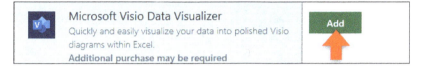

After installation, look for a new tab or group in the ribbon. Depending on the type of add-in you installed, the name of the tab or group should be related to the add-in you installed.

If not go to the 'Home' ribbon tab, then select 'add-ins'. You'll see a section at the top of the drop down menu called "my add-ins". Click on the add-in to add it to your worksheet.

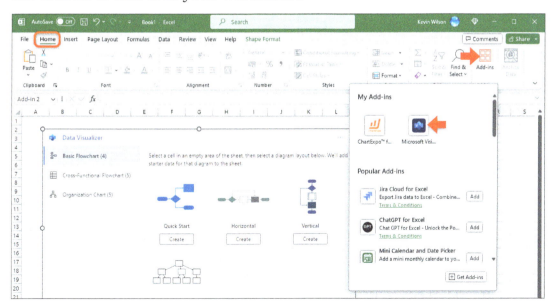

10 Macros & Automa-tion

Macros and Automation are valuable tools for automating repetitive tasks and streamlining processes.

A macro in is a recorded sequence of actions or a series of instructions created to automate repetitive or complex operations within Excel. These operations can include tasks like formatting, data manipulation, and calculations.

Some macros are created by recording a sequence of user actions within Excel. These recorded actions are then saved as a macro, and you can play them back to automate the same series of actions.

Macros can also be created using the Visual Basic for Applications (VBA) programming language. With VBA, you have more control and flexibility to create complex automation routines, perform calculations, and interact with Excel's objects using VBA code.

You'll need to download the source files from:

elluminetpress.com/excel

Macros

Let's take a look at how we can use macros to automate some of the more mundane tasks in Excel.

Recording a Macro

Let's assume we have some sales data and we want to record a macro that will automatically format the columns, cell alignments, number formats and headings.

From the 'view' ribbon tab, click the small arrow underneath 'macros'. Select 'record macro' from the drop down menu.

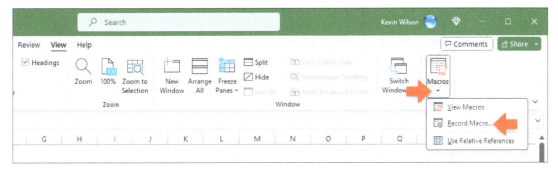

In the 'record macro' dialog box, give your macro a meaningful name. For example "FormatSalesData". Store it in "This Workbook".

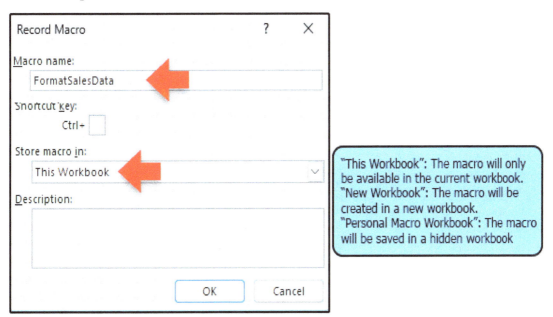

Add a keyboard shortcut if you need to. Click 'ok'.

Chapter 10: Macros & Automation

Now, perform the following actions required to process and format the sales data.

1. Set the column widths.

2. Select the headers (cells A1:C1). From the 'Home' ribbon tab, select the 'bold' icon for the headers.

3. Select cells A1:C3, then apply 'all borders' to the selected cells.

4. Select A2:A6, and set the number format to date, also align the text to the left.

5. Align C1 to the right.

6. Select cell C2:C3, and set the number format to currency.

7. Go to the 'view' ribbon tab, click 'macros', then select 'stop recording'.

Once you've recorded the macro, you can add it to your quick access toolbar on the top left of the screen. To do this click the down arrow to the right of the toolbar, select 'more commands'.

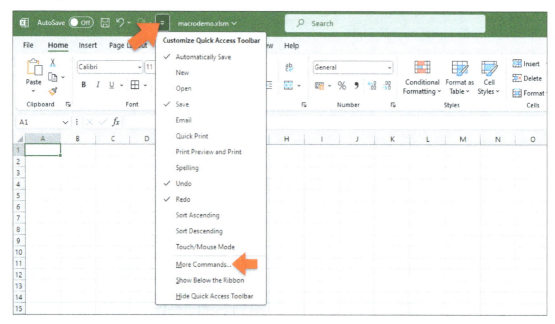

In the 'choose commands from' drop down menu at the top of the dialog box, select 'macros'.

Add the macro to the toolbar as shown below. Click 'ok' when you're done.

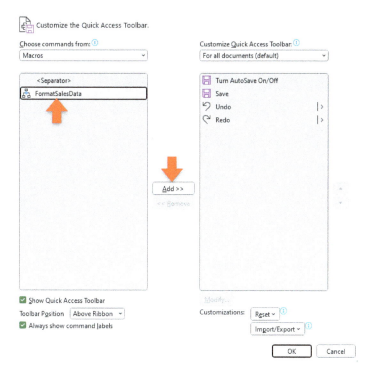

You'll find the macro appear on the quick access toolbar

Running a Macro

To run the macro we recorded in the previous section. From the 'view' ribbon tab, click the small arrow underneath 'macros'. Select 'view macros' from the drop down menu.

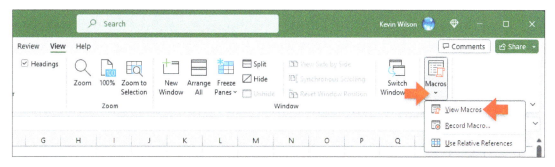

Here you'll see various options to manage and run your macros.

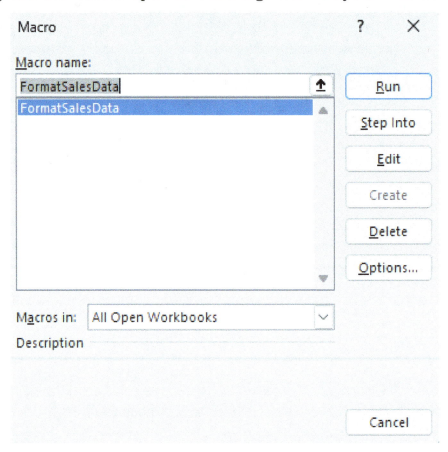

Run executes the selected macro.

Step Into opens the Visual Basic for Applications (VBA) editor and goes to the code of the selected macro, allowing you to run it line by line for debugging purposes.

Edit opens the VBA editor and takes you directly to the code of the selected macro, allowing you to modify it.

Create opens the VBA editor and creates a new macro.

Delete deletes the selected macro after prompting you for confirmation.

Options opens a dialog box where you can set options for the selected macro, such as assigning it a shortcut key or providing a description.

Macros in allows you to choose where Excel should look for macros. Options typically include "All Open Workbooks," "This Workbook," and possibly other open workbooks.

To run the macro, select it from the 'macro name' list, then click 'run'.

If you added the macro to your quick access toolbar, you'll see an icon.

Here we have another unformatted sales report for the following month. Instead of going through all the formatting steps again, we can simply use the macro.

Select the cells, click on the macro icon.

	A	B	C
1	Date	Book	Sales
2	44931	Book A	223
3	44932	Book B	444
4	44933	Book C	453
5	44934	Book D	121
6	44935	Book E	232

Here, the formatting has been applied by the macro.

	A	B	C
1	Date	Book	Sales
2	05/01/2023	Book A	£223.00
3	06/01/2023	Book B	£444.00
4	07/01/2023	Book C	£453.00
5	08/01/2023	Book D	£121.00
6	09/01/2023	Book E	£232.00

Have a look at macrodemo.xlsm

Visual Basic for Applications (VBA)

Visual Basic for Applications (VBA) is a programming language that is tightly integrated with Excel, allowing you to automate tasks, create custom forms, develop macros, and build complex data processing functions.

VBA is an event-driven programming language that's built into Excel and other Office Applications. It's complete with a built-in Integrated Development Environment (IDE) allowing you to create automated tasks and functions in the Office suite.

Chapter 10: Macros & Automation

Let's create a VBA macro that automates the process of formatting a data range in Excel. This example will demonstrate how to highlight cells based on their values, apply number formatting, and adjust column widths.

Have a look at VBADemo.xlsm

To start, go to the 'developer' ribbon tab, click on 'visual basic'. See "Developer Tab" on page 181 for information on how to enable it. This opens the VBA editor.

To write a VBA Macro, go to the 'insert' menu, then select 'module'.

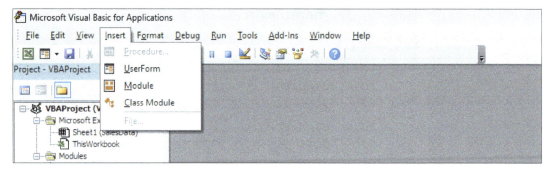

A blank window will appear allowing you to enter your VBA code to create your macro.

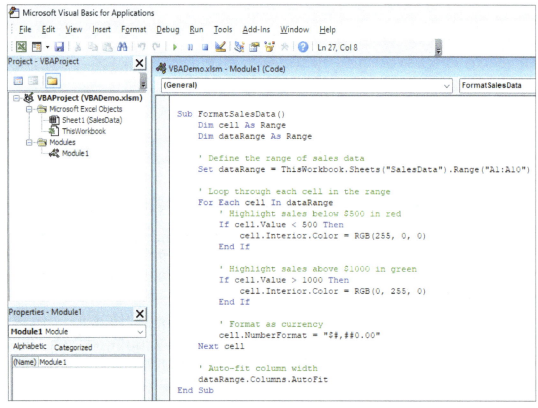

```
Sub FormatSalesData()
    Dim cell As Range
    Dim dataRange As Range

    ' Define the range of sales data
    Set dataRange = ThisWorkbook.Sheets("SalesData").Range("A1:A10")

    ' Loop through each cell in the range
    For Each cell In dataRange
        ' Highlight sales below $500 in red
        If cell.Value < 500 Then
            cell.Interior.Color = RGB(255, 0, 0)
        End If

        ' Highlight sales above $1000 in green
        If cell.Value > 1000 Then
            cell.Interior.Color = RGB(0, 255, 0)
        End If

        ' Format as currency
        cell.NumberFormat = "$#,##0.00"
    Next cell

    ' Auto-fit column width
    dataRange.Columns.AutoFit
End Sub
```

To run the macro, close the VBA editor. From the 'developer' ribbon tab, click on 'macros'. From the dialog box, select the macro, then click 'run'.

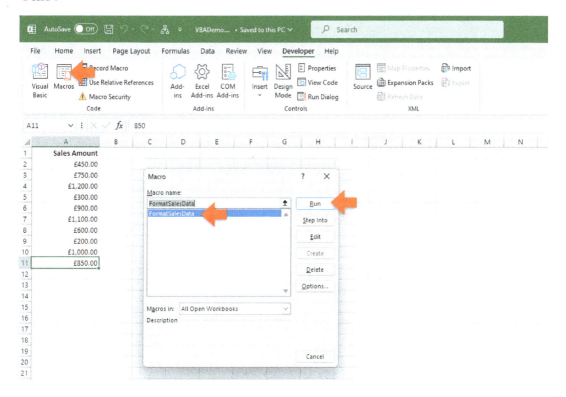

Developer Tab

The developer tab provides access to tools and functions used for creating, managing, and executing macros, as well as for developing applications using Visual Basic for Applications (VBA). It is not displayed by default in Excel, but you can easily add to the ribbon.

To do this, go to 'file'.

Click on 'options' from the bottom of the list on the left hand side.

Account

Feedback

Options

Select 'customize ribbon'. Select 'main tabs' from the 'customise the ribbon' drop down menu, then click the 'developer' checkbox. Click 'ok' when you're done.

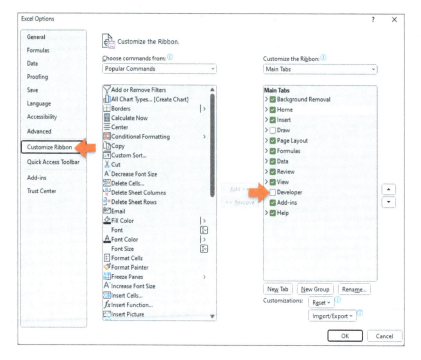

You'll see a new tab appear on the ribbon.

Visual Basic opens the Visual Basic for Applications (VBA) editor, where you can write, edit, and manage VBA code.

Macros displays a list of available macros, allowing you to run, create, edit, or delete macros.

Record Macro starts the macro recording function, allowing you to record a sequence of actions in Excel that can be replayed later as a macro.

Use Relative References toggles between using relative and absolute references while recording a macro.

Macro Security allows you to configure the security settings for macros.

Add-Ins provides options to manage and access various Excel add-ins.

Excel Add-ins opens a dialog box to manage Excel-specific add-ins.

COM Add-ins opens a dialog box to manage COM add-ins, which are add-ins developed in other programming languages.

Insert allows you to insert Form controls (like buttons, checkboxes, etc.) and ActiveX controls into your Excel workbook.

Design Mode toggles design mode on or off, allowing you to edit or interact with controls in your workbook.

Properties opens the properties window for the selected control in the VBA editor, allowing you to change its properties.

View Code opens the VBA editor and displays the code for the selected control or the worksheet, allowing you to write or edit VBA code associated with it.

Source opens thc XML Source task pane, which helps in managing XML maps and working with XML data.

Map Properties views or modifies XML property map.

Expansion Packs provides options to manage expansion packs for Excel, although this feature is less commonly used in recent versions of Excel.

Refresh Data is used to refresh the data in your Excel workbook that is connected to an external data source, including XML maps.

Insert Control provides a quick way to insert a control into your Excel workbook.

Import is used to import XML data into your Excel workbook.

Export is used to export data from your Excel workbook to an XML file.

Resources

To help you understand the procedures and concepts explored in this book, we have developed some video resources and app demos for you to use, as you work through the book.

To find the resources, open your web browser and navigate to the following website

`elluminetpress.com/excel`

At the beginning of each chapter, you'll find a website that contains the resources for that chapter.

File Resources

To save the files into your OneDrive documents folder, right click on the icons above and select 'save target as' (or 'save link as', on some browsers). In the dialog box that appears, select 'OneDrive', click the 'Documents' folder, then click 'save'.

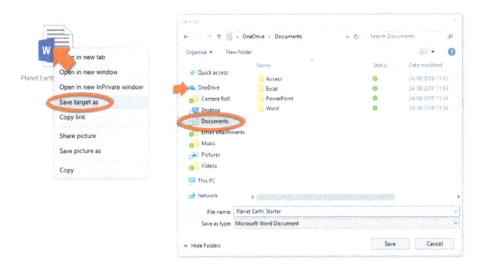

The sample images are stored in a compressed zip file. To download the zip file, right click on the zip icon on the page above, 'Sample Images.zip. Select 'save target as' (or 'save link as', on some browsers) and save it into 'pictures' on your OneDrive folder.

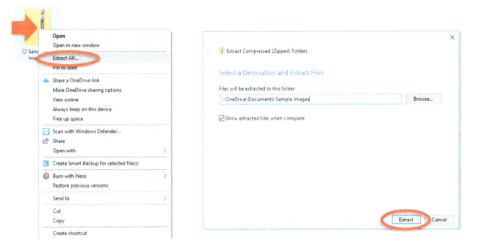

Once you have downloaded the zip file, go to your 'pictures' folder in your OneDrive, right click on the zip file, and select 'extract all' from the menu. From the dialog box that appears click 'extract'. This will create a new folder in your pictures called 'sample images'. You'll find the images used in the examples in the books.

Video Resources

The video resources are grouped into sections for each chapter in the book. Click the thumbnail link to open the section.

When you open the link to the video resources, you'll see a thumbnail list at the bottom.

Click on the thumbnail for the particular video you want to watch. Most videos are between 30 and 60 seconds outlining the procedure, others are a bit longer.

When the video is playing, hover your mouse over the video and you'll see some controls...

Let's take a look at the video controls. On the left hand side:

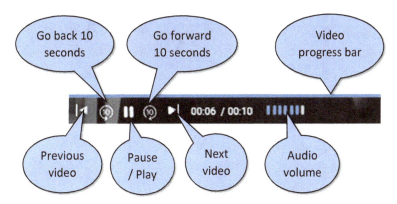

On the right hand side:

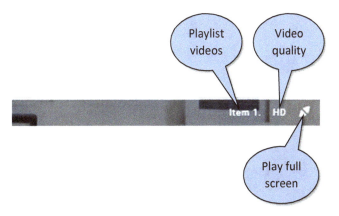

Scanning the Codes

At the beginning of each chapter, you'll a QR code you can scan with your phone to access additional resources, files and videos.

iPhone

To scan the code with your iPhone/iPad, open the camera app.

Frame the code in the middle of the screen. Tap on the website popup at the top.

Android

To scan the code with your phone or tablet, open the camera app.

Frame the code in the middle of the screen. Tap on the website popup at the top.

If it doesn't scan, turn on 'Scan QR codes'. To do this, tap the settings icon on the top left. Turn on 'scan QR codes'.

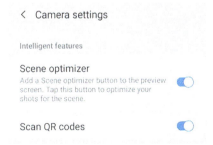

If the setting isn't there, you'll need to download a QR Code scanner. Open the Google Play Store, then search for "QR Code Scanner".

Index

Index

SOMETHING NOT COVERED?

We want to create the best possible resources to help you learn and get things done, so if we've missed anything out, then please get in touch using the links below and let us know. Thanks.

 office@elluminetpress.com

 elluminetpress.com/feedback